LONELY PLANET
UNPACKED

Travel disaster stories by Tony Wheeler
and other Lonely Planet authors

LONELY PLANET PUBLICATIONS
Melbourne • Oakland • London • Paris

Lonely Planet Unpacked: Travel disaster stories by Tony Wheeler and other Lonely Planet authors

Published by Lonely Planet Publications
    Head Office: PO Box 617, Hawthorn, Vic 3122, Australia
    Branches: 150 Linden Street, Oakland, CA 94607, USA
               10a Spring Place, London NW5 3BH, UK
               1 rue Dahomey, 75011, Paris, France

Published 1999

Printed by SNP Printing Pte Ltd, Singapore

Map by Tony Fankhauser
Designed by Jane Hart
Edited by Janet Austin

National Library of Australia Cataloguing in Publication Data

Lonely planet unpacked.

ISBN 1 86450 062 X.

1. Humorous stories. 2. Travel – Anecdotes.
I. Wheeler, Tony, 1946-.

A823.010803

Text © Lonely Planet 1999
Map © Lonely Planet 1999

Contents

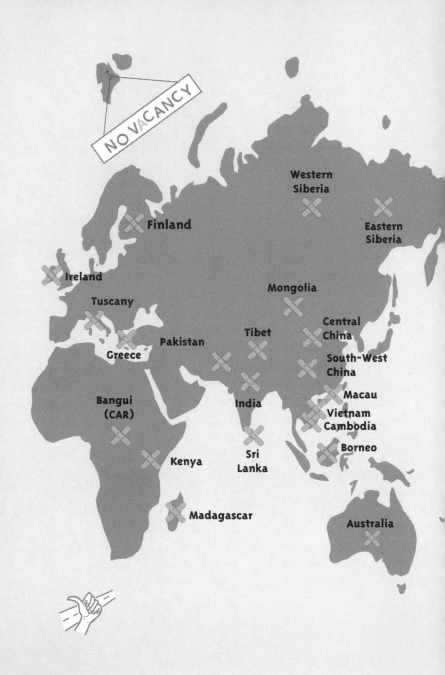

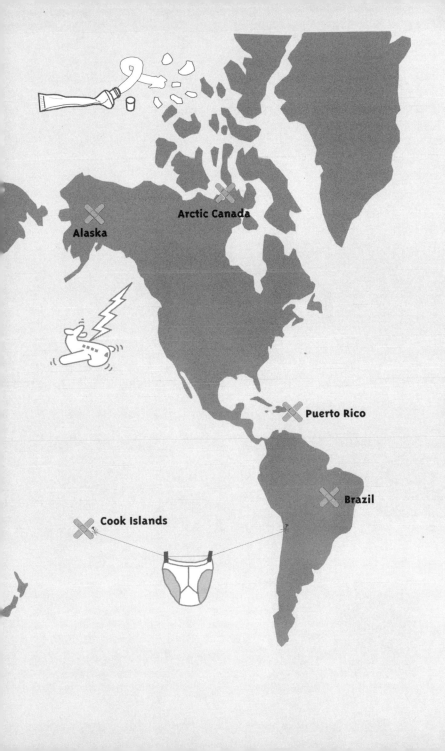

Crash

Dani Valent

Working for Lonely Planet has prevented Dani from sailing across the Atlantic on a dog trampoline, mapping the human genome and hosting her own cooking show (*Oh Naughty Wok*). Other than that, she doesn't reckon it's too bad. Dani supports native title for Australia's Aborigines and the Carlton Football Club.

YOU know how this ends. I got home alive. But when the car stopped rolling, heaved, and then sat, dreadfully silent and tangled way off the road, I hadn't known what was going to happen.

We were three days into an outback road trip. I'd borrowed a friend's dinky four-wheel drive, loaded it up with stuff, my housemate Dave, his Dutch girlfriend Lotte, and her friend Linda, and driven west, skirting Adelaide, to spend the night in rough-as-guts Port Augusta. Next day we'd driven 500 kilometres or so north till we hit Coober Pedy. It's a gem and gimmick town, so hot that a lot of houses are hacked into the ground. We spent a day there, listlessly looking at opals and being hassled by bored locals, before pondering our map and choosing a dirt track arrowing east into the desert. It was 120 kilometres to the next settlement, an Aboriginal outstation where we could camp and fill up on bore water. We were assured that the people there could point out the road onward to the Oodnadatta Track, which we thought we might follow up north to the Simpson Desert.

We filled up with petrol and Kool Mints. I was driving, and I was happy. This was the real journey – an empty rutted road, flat red desert left right in front and behind, and the wind pouring in the windows. Dave, in the front seat, talked expansively to the Dutch girls, explaining things I guessed he'd read on cereal boxes. I joined in – we were acting more Aussie than we'd ever been, breathing Vegemite and bush lore. We told them how kangaroos were born, and stories of explorers (mixing, if I recall, the adventures of Burke and Wills with the trials of Amundsen on his way to the South Pole). They probably knew better, having already told us at dinner the night before about the federation of Australia, but they let us waffle on, our accents getting broader by the kilometre. I think I even said 'strewth' and I'm sure Dave said 'fair dinkum', things we'd surely never heard anyone say in real life.

We were about an hour out of Coober Pedy, halfway to the out-station, taking a sandy hill at eighty kilometres an hour when it gave way to a bend, invisible till it was upon us. The car started skipping sideways, nothing to do with me. I felt I was righting it, working with the skid like a true-blue Aussie sheila, when the steering wheel dialled out of my hand, and in a blink, the car launched into a roll. A big skipping jaunty roll. A twisty airborne roll. A triple roll which went on for a long long time, and when it stopped we all breathed out and noticed that no-one had died.

Slowly we got out, very grateful, very scared. We picked our-selves out of the car limb by limb, counting to four and feeling lucky. We talked to one another gathering brief facts, getting assurances that we were all indeed OK. Dave was the only one with blood on him; a cut leg, not too bad. The roof rack was fifty metres along the road, debris and our gear strewn along the ground in between. We sat on the ground, flattened by shock and the gravity of our situation. We were about sixty kilometres from help in either direction. We hadn't seen one other car on the road. We'd passed no water, no crossroad, no building and certainly no emergency phone. I felt badly guilty but was too scared to ask if the others all blamed me.

Lotte and Linda were all for taking a bottle of water and walk-ing back to town, but Dave and I talked them out of it, juicing up news stories about people in exactly our position who'd been found dead of thirst just out of sight of their cars. We said it was essential that we all keep together.

We became organised, in a mechanical kind of way. An inven-tory was taken: we had food for three big camp-site meals (steaks and potatoes and corn and pumpkin and puddings in cans). A bag of oranges, ten litres of water, some biscuits, a wad of pot, Kool Mints.

Water was the most serious problem. What we had might stretch for a couple of hot, thirsty days, but it seemed quite likely we could wait a week for a rescue car. So we started pissing in bottles, building up an emergency reservoir. Dave and Lotte wanted to combine our piss; Linda and I were all for four separate stashes. But our cup never threatened to runneth over – Dave was the only one who was able to catch much of his flow in the narrow-necked litre bottle we'd recently emptied of lemonade.

I dug a hole in the lee of the car, scooping out hot sand and then cooler sand, almost wet. Could we wring out the sand somehow? Suck on it? I foresaw a dramatic death: having lost my mind, troubled and forsaken explorer-style, I sucked on sand and choked. I surveyed the shimmering red plain – there wasn't even a tree on which I could carve my initials.

As I continued to dig, images from a school camp came to mind – a bushcraft lesson in collecting water with a plastic bag, a leaf . . . wasn't there string involved somehow? Then I looked at my thighs – big Aussie hams compared to the Dutch girls' pegs – and recalled a story about Antarctic explorers who'd eaten their dogs, saving the heads till last. Most nutritious, those vitamin-rich doggy brains. I should be eaten first – the guilty driver, the fleshiest.

The Dutch girls were looking at me, not looking hungry at all.

'Of course,' I said, 'we can collect water using leaves and string before we have to drink Dave's piss.'

Lotte and Linda looked fairly impressed.

We put our food and drink into the hole and set about collecting some wood. There wasn't much of it – just scratchy saltbush twigs and stray windborne grass – but we put it all in a pile which immediately blew away. We raced after it and chucked it into the car.

Oh the car. Georgie's lovely little city four-wheel drive, generously lent to us, to me really. And now terribly terribly undeniably dead. Dave and Lotte had taped garbage bags to the shattered windows, and they thrashed in the wind. The car looked like a crippled metal bird, pathetically trying to fly away. Could we somehow make hot-air balloons out of garbage bags? I wondered idly, a desert Houdini with mush for brain. We cleared the glass from the car, making a pile like a midden on the edge of the road. Now one of us could at least sit on the back seat, as long as their head was cocked at forty-five degrees and they didn't mind head-butting the splayed seat in front.

I kept sneaking glances at the car, the rude canned shell of it. We all kept saying how lucky we were, while peering hopefully and scared this way then that along the burning, empty road.

Dave and I levered the mashed bonnet open with the tyre iron and peered inside as if it were an attic inhabited by ghosts. Like the very worst of backyard, arse-up mechanics, we scratched our heads and muttered. I looked for the fan belt, because I knew – probably from an episode of *Neighbours* – that it could be replaced with a stocking. A Dutch girl could surely be relied upon to have pantyhose. Unfortunately, the fan belt was intact, though the fan was leering wildly at the fuel pump and everything else seemed pretty bent out of shape. And, as Linda pointed out, it didn't much matter about the engine when anyone could see that the wheels on the left side of the car were flat to the ground while still being somehow attached to the axle.

Maddeningly, the radio worked.

'Can't we swap the wires over and broadcast our location?' I asked Dave.

He looked at me witheringly. 'Maybe I'll just find the frequency and play an SOS on my guitar.'

All of us kept thinking we heard cars. The wind made shapes in the desert, rushing along corridors we couldn't see, slamming doors and scurrying up lonely looking birds. It sounded like trucks, cars, whole motorcades of illusion coming to rescue us at our brave little crash site.

An orange was quartered and we ate it seriously, licking the juice that ran down our dusty arms. We'd crashed late morning and now it was late afternoon. Time, we decided, to get the tents up and think about dinner.

Our recipe was Dutch discipline blended with faux Australian bush skills. Linda divided the food into nine doll's-house portions and thought about meals which could be prepared with limited cooking; Lotte chopped the vegies into small chunks and hacked a steak into four meagre portions. Dave started a fire and Lotte and Linda whacked the food onto it. I found a rock and put it into the fire, then mashed up balls of flour and water to make chapatis.

I felt quite the tandoori master till I rolled the rock out of the fire and it crumbled into steaming mud and clay, extinguishing fingers of precious fire in the process. I gathered up my sad little flaky discs and rolled them back into one single mass.

'Let's have damper,' I said brightly, dumping it in the flames, where the outside quickly charcoaled and the inside stayed resolutely gooey. Linda kindly decided this was dessert. We ate it sprinkled with sugar and soon all had stomach aches decent enough to distract us from our predicament.

After an ominous sunset, it became cold very quickly. As we'd decided not to use the torch except in necessity, there wasn't much to do but lie with swollen stomachs in two tents. I hated myself, went to sleep and dreamt about when I was little and had a paper round, and was persecuted by girls from the private school on my route. All teeth and pigtails, they stole my newspapers, hid my trolley and pulled my hair. This night I felt well deserving of punishment and woke up shivering in the night, scared, sad and lonely, fearing alley cats in prim blue-and-white check.

My paper-round money had paid for a stereo which was still in my bedroom. I supposed my sister could have it if I died. I worried that I hadn't made a will. I worried about my parents reading my diary. I wondered how long it would be before people started looking for us.

The morning dawned bleak and beautiful and hopeless. I got up, peeled off a sweaty layer, and launched into a few yoga moves with what I hoped was optimism.

Lotte and Linda were boiling up a billy for some tea and had laid out some cereal. Dave sat next to Lotte rolling a breakfast joint.

'You look like a tangled emu,' Dave said helpfully as I sat in a complicated side-twist which ensured sand lodged in my buttocks.

'Quite the naturalist, aren't you?' I bit back, displaying a shameful lack of karmic alignment.

I couldn't remember any more yoga, so I bowed in the general direction of the sun and went to sit with the others. I thought about making scones, but couldn't find the flour and suspected it had been hidden from me, the Damper Villain. Fair enough.

In a way it was just like any camping trip with friends. We had camped in a stupid place, had all been bitten by things we couldn't see, and had the inevitable discussion about whether ants got hurt when they fell. Last time I'd debated the matter I'd argued that ants could turn themselves into tiny parachutes, spreading their legs and touching down gently. This time, feeling death closer at hand, I leadenly insisted that many an ant suffered a broken back or a snapped leg in the tumble from human height to land level.

The teasing wind-car noises started up again after breakfast, and then, as ordinary as socks, a real van came at us from the right. First we watched it blinking, then we stood up and ran towards it, arms like windmills. It stopped and a tall Aboriginal priest with silver hair got out and folded his arms.

'You all OK?' he asked levelly.

'Yes, yes, we're fine.'

'Not another one left in the car?'

'No, no, just the four of us.'

'Very lucky.'

Indeed. The rest of the day was all driving, cops, tow trucks and reconstructions. We booked a motel room for the night and bus tickets south for the morning. I practised a serious jaws-of-death tone of voice and planned my phone call to the suddenly car-less Georgie. Strewth.

The first hour of the first day of my first assignment for Lonely Planet

Miles Roddis

Always an avid devourer and user of guidebooks, Miles came late to contributing to them. For more than twenty-five years he lived, worked, walked and ran in eight countries, including Laos, Iran, Spain and Egypt. He celebrated a new life by cycling 20,000 kilometres around the rim of the USA. Convinced that the bike is humankind's greatest invention (other than Velcro), he enjoys agitating for cyclists' rights and annoying motorists. Now settled in Spain, he writes for outdoor and athletics magazines, and despite his distressing first day with Lonely Planet he has contributed to *Africa on a shoestring*, *Walking in Britain*, *West Africa* and *Walking in France*, and was coordinating author of *Walking in Spain*.

I T'S not easy to wedge your big toe through Lonely Planet's door, knowing full well that every month dozens of other aspirant travel writers are trying to do just the same. So when you're finally granted an assignment, you don't bargain, wheedle and assert your preference for Bhutan, Bali or a few of the more laid-back Caribbean islands.

Thus it was that I found myself on an Air France jumbo, wedged between a Belgian agricultural engineer of mastodon proportions and a mammoth Congolese student heading home after studies in Paris. The night flight had left me terminally jet-lagged, my head awhirl with a thousand and more details from the previous Lonely Planet writer's lowdown. And, as my soggy brain managed to tell me, I was decidedly wet behind the ears from much more than the pre-dawn shave and cold water which I'd sluiced over my face in an attempt to shake myself out of a deep torpor.

I squinted through the plane's porthole as it began its descent towards Bangui airport. Before you reach for your atlas – as I had done, barely a couple of weeks earlier – I'll tell you; it's the capital of the Central African Republic, abbreviated in everyday speech to CAR. Or rather, it's what remains of the capital. The CAR army at that time had a distressing tendency to march unannounced out of their barracks, shooting from hip and howitzer to wreak their impressive worst on the town.

The Central African Republic and Chad – the one subject to regular army putsches, the other seemingly engaged in perpetual civil war; such were my first two experiences of life writing for Lonely Planet. Only in retrospect, much later, did I realise the collective sigh of editorial relief that must have wafted through the company's Melbourne office at the news that some mug had at last been signed up to cover the two countries.

Bangui, the few friends who had heard of the place assured me, rivalled Lagos, Nairobi and Abidjan in the quality and quantity of its urban violence. In the words of the very guidebook which I'd been commissioned to update, 'Bangui is a city of thieves and pickpockets. Stay clear of groups of young men. If you go out at night, never walk.'

Welcome to Bangui. As the jumbo began its swoop over the town's small airport, I picked out the armoured cars flanking the runway, each with its platoon of French soldiers wearing a khaki version of those briefest of thigh-hugging shorts that only the French still go in for these days. And each with a large gun mounted and trained towards the skies.

More gun-toting, short shorts-sporting *soldats* patrolled the arrivals area, where the customs officer discreetly signalled to me that if I equally discreetly made a modest unreceipted payment to his companion, my backpack would pass through without inspection. I affected incomprehension and, in their need to work quickly and profitably through the queue of travellers at my back, they waved me through. Ha! A first tiny triumph.

Few are the travellers who manage the journey between airport and town in Third World countries without being savagely ripped off. But, armed with my guidebook, I knew the reasonable tariff and came out guns blazing, ready for a spot of hard bargaining. Funny that, I mused, as the most assertive taxi driver pulled his battered vehicle away from the arrivals area; funny that I couldn't get a single driver to budge below four times the top rate the guidebook had quoted.

Many are the travellers at airports throughout the world who, because of the persuasive powers of their commission-hungry taxi driver, fetch up at a hotel other than the one of their choice. But I was made of sterner stuff. 'Hôtel Minerva,' I insisted, mindful of Lonely Planet's assessment: 'the only hotel which might possibly be within your price range'.

'*N'existe plus, chef,*' insisted my driver. It's not there any more.

I affected incomprehension once again and, in the manner of tourists when ill at ease, repeated my injunction a couple of decibels louder. '*HÔTEL MINERVA, s'il vous PLAÎT,*' I responded, with both confidence and that ingratiating 'please' which we British feel obliged to append to any order.

'*Y'en a pas, chef.*' No such thing, boss.

Barely ten minutes and one excessively fat cab fare later (the taxi charge inflated even higher since the driver had no change for the smallest of the large-denomination French banknotes I was carrying), we pulled up outside the Hôtel Minerva. Or rather, outside the remains of the Hôtel Minerva, shot to smithereens by the army in one of its more dramatic sorties.

'*Te l'avais bien dit, chef,*' remarked the driver with a cheery leer, 'told you so. But I know another, much better, special price. This time, the ride's on me.'

Thus it was that, pausing only to note the need to revise my predecessor's assessment of the one-time Hôtel Minerva, I fetched up in a hotel so expensive as to be way beyond consideration for Lonely Planet's *Africa on a shoestring* – or indeed of any but the most profligate travel writer.

I patiently waited my turn until the protracted negotiations between the receptionist and my driver over his commission were concluded, apparently to neither party's satisfaction. The latter headed mumbling for the street clutching a wad of grimy notes which the former had produced from under the desk. I resisted the receptionist's resistible offer to sell me a dog-eared copy of the collected thoughts of the dead and discredited Emperor Bokassa for the equivalent of a mere US$60. I also registered the fact that I appeared to be the hotel's only guest and, more urgently, that Bangui was about to embark upon three days of national holiday; shops and banks were closing imminently and I hadn't a single Central African franc to my name.

In the privacy of my room, I hurriedly peeled off a few high-denomination French banknotes, scribbled a quick shopping list, grabbed my passport, rammed everything into my pockets and dashed for the door. Heedful of that warning about crime levels, I walked briskly and purposefully in the direction of item 68 on my map of downtown Bangui, side vision keen and mindful of my back.

Hugging the very middle of the muddy, traffic-free road, I began to get a grip on the town. I noted en passant that item 62, Novotel Bangui, was but a shell; No 54, a modest grocery store, had been torched; and No 61, the Pharmacie Centrale, was gutted. More worryingly, only the twisted girders of item 56, the BCAD bank, remained as witness of the army's latest rampage. And all this since the last Lonely Planet edition and the one I was here to revise.

But amid the destruction, item 68, the solid concrete mass of the BEAC bank, was reassuringly intact, if you ignored a pockmark or two. I mounted its crowded steps, squeezed my way in and picked a passage to the foreign exchange counter, before which, with barely ten minutes to closing time, an attempt at a queue seethed and swelled.

I briefly assessed my position. Here I stood, profoundly jet-lagged, overheated, pasty mouthed, knowing not a soul in town and without a single centime in local currency. Stuck at the end of the scrum, the only non-national in line, my chances of getting any cash were receding with each tick of those ten minutes. With everyone else about to go on extended holiday, I was preparing to begin a job I'd never done before. Why the hell was I here? I asked myself.

A kind Centrafricain interrupted this self-indulgent reverie, beckoning to me and insisting, despite my half-hearted protestations, that I should slip in front of him, so gaining several places over the mildly protesting back markers.

The mass surged up to and around the window, behind which sat a particularly surly teller. Snarling at the crowd, he would occasionally and arbitrarily grab a paper from the hand of one of the insurgents as the wave of people passed before his booth. But my new-found friend graciously protected me with his body, propelling me gently forward and remonstrating with his compatriots. Whispering the while into my ear his regrets at their uncouthness, he wished me greater good fortune during the rest of my stay as an honoured guest in his country.

Finally, one of the surges propelled me in front of the window, which I grabbed to prevent myself being swept back by the ebb.

The teller snatched my passport and I knew that I'd entered the system, that money might well be mine and that I could temporarily relax.

As I turned to thank my protector for his solicitousness towards a visitor, I saw him heading at speed for the main exit. I reached instinctively for my back pocket – and found it empty, the button dexterously flicked open.

It remains one of the great regrets of my life that I wasn't present to celebrate with my erstwhile protector when he opened his fist to reveal – nothing more and nothing less than my shopping list.

Walking the Mount Kailash circuit

Tony Wheeler

As the founder and principal author of Lonely Planet Publications, Tony Wheeler's advice is sought after by independent travellers all over the world. *New York Times Magazine* recently called him 'the trailblazing Patron saint of the world's backpackers and adventure travellers' (30 June 1996). In *Travel & Leisure*'s 25th Anniversary Issue (September 1996), Tony was included in the 'What's Ahead' feature as one of the people who has changed the way the world travels. Tony has helped to write a number of Lonely Planet books, including guides to Bali & Lombok, Britain, California & Nevada, Cambodia, Dublin, India, Ireland, Japan, Myanmar (Burma), Nepal, Papua New Guinea, Paris, Rarotonga & the Cook Islands, San Francisco, Singapore, South-East Asia, Sri Lanka, Tahiti & French Polynesia, and Western Europe. About the research strategy employed by Lonely Planet, Tony says: 'At Lonely Planet we like to say that our writers go to the end of the road. And they had damn well better. Because I go to the end of the road.'

BLAM! The mad Tibetan slammed his head against the windscreen with such force that cracks shot across the screen from the point of impact.

Whack! He reared back and repeated the procedure. More cracks flashed out across the screen, which now bulged ominously inwards.

Wait a minute, I thought. Surely this shouldn't be happening to me. I'm sin free. When you've just wiped out the sins of a lifetime, the last thing you expect to find is a mad Tibetan trying to climb in the car with you – through the front windscreen.

It must have been 1980 when I first heard of Mount Kailash, and although I was unaware of its sin-washing potential at the time, it was instantly filed on my 'I'd like to go there' list. I'd been staying just outside Pahalgam in Kashmir, and every day hordes of Indian pilgrims had passed by on their way up to Amarnath, where each year a sacred column of ice would appear in a remote cave. It was no mere frozen stalagmite which inspired thousands of worshippers to make the tough trek north. No, the icy phallic symbol was exactly that – a manifestation of Shiva's lingam, the very penis of the Hindu faith's great creator and destroyer. Not too far from this important Shiva site was an even more significant location: Mount Kailash, the comfortable residence of Lord Shiva and his gorgeous partner Parvati. The only trouble with Shiva's mountain-top home was that it was on the wrong side of the Himalaya, north of the main range in Tibet. And back in 1980, Mao and his mates weren't exactly putting the welcome mat out.

Then things changed. China opened up a little, and a bit later Tibet as well. Soon intrepid travellers were finding their way to the furthest corners of the Tibetan Autonomous Region, as the

Chinese dubbed the controversial country. There could hardly be a more remote corner of the world than Mount Kailash, tucked away in Tibet's wild west. It has always been that way. Mount Kailash has been a magnet for Hindu, Buddhist, Jain and Bönpo (followers of the ancient pre-Buddhist religion known as Bön) pilgrims for centuries, but getting there has never been easy. Today there may be no bandits waiting in ambush but there's still no simple way of approaching the holy mountain. Getting to the base of the mountain means a week's drive over lousy roads or, as we did, a similar spell on foot from the nearest mountain airstrip in the far west of Nepal.

Nor is merely getting to the foot of the mountain the end of the matter. Having arrived, you now have to walk around the mountain, to perform a *kora* if you're Buddhist, a *parikrama* if you're Hindu. The fifty-kilometre circuit is a one-day sprint if you're a typically enthusiastic Tibetan Buddhist; a more leisurely three- or four-day stroll if you're a Hindu pilgrim with the odd holy lake demanding a ritual submersion along the way. The latest pilgrims, the Western ones, also opt for the three- or four-day circuit.

On a crystal-clear, sunny day in early September we set out from Darchen, the grubby little jumping-off point to the south of the mountain. We were a big group: six Westerners, a Sherpa trekking crew we'd brought up with us from Nepal and no fewer than thirteen yaks to cart our tents, camping equipment and supplies. This was *kora* luxury, but it was no wonder the air was so crystal clear – there wasn't much of it. Even our starting point was at 4560 metres, and by the time we topped the Drölma-la pass on the other side of the mountain we'd be at 5630 metres, up at Everest Base Camp altitude.

Only an hour into the walk we came to the *kora*'s first *chaktsal gang* or 'prostration point'. Here, pilgrims – and trekkers too, if they're determined to get into the spirit of things – sprawl flat out on the ground, hands pointed like a springboard diver towards the holy mountain. Of course, if you're a very enthusiastic Tibetan pilgrim, the first prostration point will not actually be the site for your first prostration. No, the real enthusiasts prostrate themselves for the whole fifty-kilometre circuit! This does, of course, take a little longer than the usual *kora* stroll. Count on three weeks if you're contemplating making a flat-on-your-face circuit of the holy mountain.

Back on our feet we strolled on to the Tarboche, a gigantic prayer flagpole erected during the mountain's major annual festival, Saga Dawa. Tibetans may put a great deal of effort into prayer and pilgrimage, but they economise wherever possible; prayer flags are one of the most visible signs of this efficiency drive. Print a prayer or mantra on a flag and with each windy flap the prayer is carried away to the heavens. Red, white and green prayer flags can be seen strung across mountain passes and flying above monasteries right across Tibet.

Beyond the Tarboche's enormous prayer flag collection we entered the spectacular Lha Chu valley, running along the western side of the mountain. We lunched beside the valley's swift-flowing river, made a short side trip to visit the hillside Chuku Monastery, then spent the rest of the afternoon walking north, the west or ruby face of Mount Kailash brooding above us.

There was ice on our tent next morning and groups of Tibetan pilgrims were already striding resolutely past us along the opposite bank of the river. Swinging their prayer wheels as they marched, they had left Darchen before dawn, in order to complete their circuit in one long day. Once the sun had crept above the mountain we soon defrosted and recommenced the *kora*. We waded across the icy Dunglung Chu, cascading down from a side valley, and passed a head-high stone carved with the sacred Tibetan mantra *Om Mani Padme Hum*: 'Hail to the Jewel in the Lotus'. Late morning found us picnicking below the *kora*'s second monastery, Dira-puk.

It was only an hour's climb beyond the monastery to our second night's camp site at 5210 metres. Any higher could have presented us with problems; some of our group were already complaining of headaches, an early sign of altitude discomfort. That extra bit of height would, however, make the next day's ascent of the Drölma-la an easier proposition. The north face of Mount

Kailash towered directly above our camp site, only a stone's throw away, and a couple of us spent the afternoon walking up to the glacier tumbling down from the face, a short and furious snowstorm coating us white.

It was even colder the next morning, but fortunately sunlight covered us before we'd even finished breakfast and the steady climb towards the pass soon thawed us out. There was plenty to be seen on the ascent. First we came to Shiva-tsal, where pilgrims envision their death and subsequent rebirth. Leaving an item of clothing at the site symbolises the casting off of one life and the preparation for the next, and as a result Shiva-tsal looks like a huge open-air second-hand clothes market. As we carried on uphill I glanced back at my spider underpants, draped across a rock. Maureen had always said they were a clear indication of my childish bad taste.

We soon came to Bardo Trang, the sin-testing stone. Walking around Kailash is said to wipe out all the sins of your lifetime. A serious sin cleansing, however, wiping out all the sins of *all* your lifetimes, takes a much larger commitment: a ticket to nirvana requires 108 circuits of the mountain. Nevertheless, even a minor one-lifetime scrub up is only possible if you start out with the right attitude, and a sin-testing stone checks your karma quota. The test is simple: you just have to slide through the narrow passage under the stone. Too much sin and you'll get stuck, no matter how skinny you are. And if you have too much sin, a single circuit may simply not be enough to tidy up your life. Fortunately, I slipped through without any difficulty . . . well, perhaps my hips were just a little wider than I expected.

From there it was climb, climb, climb until the prayer-flagged saddle of the Drölma-la came into view. We relaxed in the chilly but sun-dappled air, watching a steady stream of pilgrims arrive at the pass, chanting '*Ki ki so so la gyalo,*' the traditional Tibetan pass-crossing mantra. One cheerful group of pilgrims arrived at the pass from the opposite direction, their counterclockwise circuit of the mountain confirming that they were not Buddhists but Bönpos.

Down the other side of the pass we soon came to Gouri Kund, the Lake of Compassion, where the unfortunate Hindu pilgrims are supposed to enjoy another ritual immersion, even if it requires breaking the ice before jumping in. Sensibly, the Tibetans have never held much store with this washing lark, which the Hindus are so keen on. Then it was down, down, down, traversing a lunar landscape of bare rocks and boulders, until we eventually arrived at the Lham Chu Khir, the eastern counterpart of the western side's Lha Chu valley. Halfway through lunch it began to hail, continuing on for the next hour as we trekked south down the valley, reminding us once again that correcting a lifetime's sin doesn't come easy.

That night we camped on yet another grassy riverbank; Tibet, for all its spartan hardships, had no trouble at all in turning out a succession of idyllic camp sites. The next morning we were iced in once again, but it was only a short stroll down to the final *kora* monastery, the Zutul-puk, or 'miracle cave'. Another hour's walk spilled us out of the narrowing valley on to the flat Barkha plain, from where it was just another hour or so back to our starting point, slummy Darchen.

Where our Tibetan run-in took place. Countless people were milling around in the hotel's dismal compound as we packed a truck and two Land Cruisers with our trekking gear and our Nepalese trekking crew. There were pilgrims arriving and departing, Tibetan souvenir sellers, local drivers and guides, the odd Western traveller cycling in from Kashgar, out-of-place Chinese PLA soldiers . . . and one increasingly drunken Tibetan. Staggering back and forth, beer bottle in hand, he'd become more and more abusive and unpleasant with each swig. He'd already had an altercation with one of our Nepalese crew, but then, just as we were driving off, he suddenly flipped out completely and flung himself at the car.

The windscreen bulged inwards once again with the third head butt, and when it showed no sign of giving way he reached under his jacket and pulled out a viciously large knife. We tumbled out of the car and scattered in all directions. For the next twenty minutes he ricocheted back and forth across the compound, far too drunk to catch anyone. Finally, like the cavalry riding in to save the day in a B-Western movie, the local PSB (Public Security Bureau) honcho turned up.

And shot him.

Not dead, just in the leg. When it heals up and he's let out of jail, it will probably take him a *kora* or two to sort out his supply of bad karma.

Terror and anguish on Europe's safest roads

Jennifer Brewer

Jennifer is a Los Angeles-based professional writer, photographer and artist. She did a two-year stint at a New York City fashion magazine before striking out to write for the Berkeley Guides (now defunct), which fired her passion for travel. She's since covered Central America, Europe, the Middle East and Asia, for pleasure and on assignment.

THE sun, that traitorous sun, cast an ironic shadow on the chill Tuesday in March when my rented Fiat Brava plunged into a deep ditch on a one-lane farm road just outside the town of Mariehamn, in the Åland islands – a low-lying cluster of rocks, sheep, people and pancakes that is thoroughly Swedish, and Swedish-speaking, but has been bundled with Finland since a well-intentioned 1921 League of Nations decree.

The car, a mere babe with only eight kilometres on the ticker prior to this adventure, pitched forward while emitting a series of startled honks. My reaction was far more shrill. My fear of the plunge, it seemed, was back. Nowhere was I safe.

If you've ever flipped through your city's Foreign News section you've probably seen them: the Bus Plunge articles. Short articles about fatal accidents in countries with bad roads, steep mountains and heavy dependence on transportation by bus. Invariably, these articles begin with the words 'A bus plunged . . .' and end with a quick count of the dead, usually numbering in the tens or dozens. They're terse, these Bus Plunge articles, and they always have terrible endings.

Some see in them a reckoning: how many lives must be lost on a Third World roadway for it to be considered First World news? When three Americans are slain in Venezuela, it makes front-page headlines and swallows hours of airtime on CNN. If a truck-load of people goes off a cliff in the Karakorams, it merits three lines of an AP stringer's time. Such is the way the world turns.

Whatever their larger meaning, the Bus Plunge articles have long held a certain Know-thy-enemy fascination for me. Unlike the late filmmaker Stanley Kubrick, who refused for all time to leave the terra firma of England after eavesdropping on conversations between airline pilots and air traffic controllers at La Guardia Airport in New York City, I avidly collect Bus Plunge articles. I have also been known to travel in Bus Plunge zones.

'Resolve to take Fate by the throat and shake a living out of her', wrote Louisa May Alcott in 1889, a sentiment with which my mother, my shrink and my subconscious do not always agree. And so, with dry mouth and wet palms, I have explored some of the Bus Plunge capitals of the world. One year it's been liver-splitting rides across the mud-knuckled roads of rainy-season Central and South America. The next, brisket-thumping scrambles through the ravelled mountains of northern India, Nepal and Tibet. On each trip, I have known the risks, and have lived in fear of that terrible ultimate plunge. But where the plunge was expected, the plunge never came.

According to statistics, a fatal road accident is from fifteen to twenty times more likely in India than in the United States, with the official death toll in India hovering around 65,000 annually. It's worth noting that this is the official death toll, not the accurate one; in a country of some 950 million, the true count may have fallen through the cracks.

A significant percentage of India's fatal road accidents occur on the hairpin turns and rail-less ravines of roads carved into the Himalaya, and of those, an unignorable number befall motorists on the Manali-to-Leh highway, a near-vertical track across uninhabited, craggy, mist-and-ice shrouded peaks, the second-highest motorable road in the world.

If you're a Bus Plunge junkie yearning for a chokehold on Fate's throat, this is your trip. Travel here, and toothless men will wag their heads and tell you that ten people died for each and every kilometre of road laid. Shredded flyers from embassies, with grainy passport photos and the legend 'MISSING SINCE . . .' flutter like prayer flags at lonely military checkpoint tents along the route. Banditry, people say. Fallout from the skirmishes with Muslim guerrillas from Pakistan, further north-west. But press on further and they'll shrug. That lost foreigner probably hitched a lift on one of the carnival-painted Tata trucks that deliver cornflakes and chapati flour to Ladakh from the fertile lowlands to the south, and the Tata simply slipped over a cliff. It happens.

Some stretches of the Manali-to-Leh road measure barely a jeep-and-a-half wide, with soft gravel shoulders spilling over into abrupt chasms hundreds of metres deep. One glance out of the bus window and you're dizzy. Bad brakes, bald tyres, a frown from Ganesh, and you're gone forever.

But like I said, it didn't happen to me.

In contrast, Finland is flat, very flat. During the Ice Age, a mammoth glacier covered much of Scandinavia, compressing the bedrock of present-day Finland and flattening it like an Åland pancake. Halti, the country's highest mountain, would be a pimple in the Himalaya, rising a scant 1328 metres above sea level. If undertaking a driving tour of Finland, flatness, I felt reassured, would be good. Not for nothing has a recent EU survey named Finland as having some of the safest roads in Europe.

This was the plan. Starting from the rental-car counter at Frankfurt, I would motor north to the Arctic Circle in Finnish Lapland, jump out, howl at the Midnight Sun, and then migrate south again, soaking up as much Finnish culture as I could bear along the way.

However, I would be an American of Irish extraction driving an Italian car with German licence plates in Finland, a mix that to me sounded volatile enough to start a war. There was bound to be trouble. And the trouble did not come without proper warning. Next to a ferry landing in the Åland islands, like a 'Danger: beware of the guard dog' sign posted by the proud owner of a chihuahua, was a placard that depicted a car tipping over a tiny ledge.

Ha ha, I thought. Car plunge. The sign warned against Car Plunge.

Moments later, the Fiat Brava pitched into the ditch. In the surreal *Still Life with Car* that resulted, its back wheels floated three feet off the ground. Wind whistled through the blades of a lonely red windmill in a fallow field. Sheep stared. My stomach shyly requested an Åland pancake. I scanned the road for help, but the road was empty. The sun, now a gymnast, hurdled ever higher. But my luck had fallen, my fears at last realised on one of Europe's safest roads.

Misadventure in south-west China

Tim Nollen

Tim comes from Washington, DC. After university, he settled in Prague in the early 1990s – just before it was hip, of course – teaching primary school English and dealing property on the burgeoning real estate market. He has written and updated guidebooks to several European countries for various publishers, and has had articles published on subjects as diverse as the Dead Sea, the Trans-Siberian railroad and a Czech piano manufacturer. For some reason, he currently lives in Philadelphia.

THE bus station in Wuzhou was unusually quiet. A few scattered souls lined the dirty walls, idly smoking cigarettes. A month of frenetic, exhilarating travel through China's brash hypercities had accustomed me to the usual crush of bodies in public places, but the near-suicide of rushing the ticket windows in Beijing's main station now seemed like a weird nightmare. The distilled calm in Wuzhou this Friday morning was almost unnatural.

The rigours of the road were wearing on me mightily. I longed for a spot of peace in this land of over a billion people – most of whom barely managed to pull their curious eyes away from me long enough to remember they had something they could sell me. I was tired of the daily hassles, trying to ignore the probing stares, fighting off the constant demands to buy ice-cream, used bicycle parts or caged birds. I found hope in my trusty guidebook, which described the village of Yangshuo as 'a laid-back town if there was one in China, [offering] a rare opportunity to relax and explore the villages and countryside'. A friend of mine who'd lived and travelled in China had told me that this region in the south-west was not to be missed. Even though it totalled some thirty hours from Guangzhou, my previous destination, I figured the trip was worth it.

My plan had been to take an overnight boat from Guangzhou's Pearl River dock to Wuzhou and continue on the all-day bus to Yangshuo. And in almost fictional manner, my transportation scheme went click-bam straight. It went so well, in fact, that the utterly bone-headed mistake I made, which could easily have left me completely stranded in rural China, even seemed to fit into the plan.

I managed to weave my way through the chaos of Guangzhou to the Pearl River pier. Eager to catch the early-afternoon boat, I settled for a slight ticket rip-off from a black marketeer and jumped onto the flat-bottomed barge. My cabin – probably a cargo-hold in a previous life – lay below the water line and was packed with Chinese merrymakers chattering, laughing and playing cards (all night long, as it turned out) under the insistent gloom of fluorescent lights. Ignoring the stares and the popsicles and the second-hand soft-porn magazines shoved at me, I rolled out my straw mat and rumpled bedsheet. There were thirty-two of us in the compartment: two tiers on each side, eight mats to a tier, all very efficiently laid out. The Chinese, as I was to learn the very next evening, can be brutally efficient when called upon; it just doesn't seem that way when you're in the middle of things. One of my suite-mates, an amusing fellow named Wu, laughed at my bewilderment and offered me a Lucky Strike.

Guangzhou slipped away reluctantly. Noisy commercial vessels and chugging little dinghies caused confusion in the river, and the parade of apartment blocks and factories just didn't want to give in to rurality. Eventually, though, the city relinquished its grip and we slid into delightfully bucolic scenery.

The deep orange of a fiery sunset reflected off the dirty brown river in a perfectly impressionistic moment. Again I was struck by the apparent paleness of light in China: soft baby blues and rich shades of orange spread across the sky. The river was broad and calm, with red clay banks and thick green tropical vegetation. There were very few bridges outside the big cities – only ferries. Dozens of low mini-barges plied the waters loaded with bamboo poles, steel pipes and silt from dredging operations upriver. Peasants in wide-brimmed umbrella-like straw hats squatted along the banks, villages dotted the shoreline and children jumped and swam in the murky water.

I spent part of the evening on deck, pretending to carry on a conversation with Wu while drinking hot jasmine tea from my plastic water bottle. I never would have thought how lovely hot tea could be on a muggy summer night, cold beer being unavailable. A misty fog drifted across the river, and the sky was punctuated with bursts of heat lightning, echoing far above. Wu kept grabbing my notepad from my hands, laughing at my incomprehensible handwriting and improving it with some of his own. The Chinese characters looked pretty on my page, but I had no hope of reading them.

The boat docked in Wuzhou at 10.40 the next morning, and the empty bus station next door had an old rattletrap pulling out at 11.30 for Yangshuo. Fifty minutes in Wuzhou gave me enough time to peek up a street or two and stock up on bottles of water and stale crackers for the ride. As usual, I could only estimate how long this trip was really going to take, so I asked the woman sitting undisturbed behind the ticket counter in my best phrase-book Chinese: 'When do we arrive in Yangshuo?'

'No,' she chuckled, waving her hand briskly in front of her face as if I were merely a pesky fly. I supposed I was, because I tried again.

'Yangshuo?'

'No!' I pointed to my watch and tried to keep smiling, the irritation starting to creep up the back of my neck.

'No!' and she abruptly turned aside.

At 11.20 I climbed on board the bus, relieved to see there were only two or three other people sitting inside. Maybe this would be an uneventful ride; maybe I wouldn't be a source of entertainment for everyone around me, pointing and laughing at my white face; maybe I wouldn't catch the spray of some kid in front of me puking out the window.

At 11.25 a mad rush of people suddenly smashed on board like a wicked surf, and I was confined to my sticky brown plastic seat in the ninety-degree heat of mid-morning August. I'd never perspired like this in my entire life. Sweat poured from all pores; my T-shirt and shorts were soaked through and I could feel the sweat rolling down my ankles. It was so damn hot I couldn't even stand to feel the money belt wrapped around my waist any longer, and so, ever cautious of the people around me, I tied it carefully to the luggage rack above my head.

The bus roared off, creating entirely too much commotion for the result it achieved. We slammed and blared our way through the streets of Wuzhou (local road etiquette holds that bus drivers must announce their presence when coming upon cyclists, which in most of China means buses blast away every few seconds) and out into the hills and rice paddies.

This was the China I had come to see: oxen pulling muddy ploughs, water buffaloes sunk up to their horns in muddy pools, people transporting logs on carts attached to the back of their bicycles, an overturned truck, a bus in a ditch, pigs wrapped in cloth straightjackets and piled twelve deep onto a flatbed pick-up, passengers boarding with live chickens, endless bean fields and rice paddies, low green hills poking up on the horizon and the constant exuberant horn signalling our forward progress.

We broke down more than once, more than twice – in fact, we came to a halt four or five times, but the gallant crew of two drivers made miraculous repairs on the spot. Off we would charge once again, windows a-rattling on the bumpy two-lane road, my nerves starting to feel one with the mingled heat, dust, dirt, noise and commotion.

Speed seemed to be a constant concern of the drivers: we careered around curves like there was no tomorrow, as if in a desperate attempt to reach our destination before the bus completely collapsed. One of the drivers finally seemed to realise that if he got a good start on the downhill slope he might just have enough speed to make it over the top of the next. This discovery led to an even more furious clattering pace until nightfall, when the road evened out and we flew through the dusty tropical heart unhindered.

By now I was exhausted from two straight days of grit and fuss. I sat on the edge of my seat, impatient and grumpy, wondering if it was really necessary to go through all this just to find serenity in China. At every little town we came to I asked the poor old man sitting opposite me if we were in Yangshuo yet. At dusk a series of strange, conical, rocky green hills started popping up in the distant sunset, looking more like cartoon drawings than anything real. After almost nine hours of bus travel I began to sense that the end was in sight; all I wanted was a plate of fried noodles, a big Qingdao beer, a shower and a bed.

We arrived in Yangshuo to a fanfare of noise and lights. This was it! My man across the aisle suddenly seemed as excited as I was, as the bus driver slammed on the brakes. I leapt up, grabbed my backpack and fell out of the bus and onto the doorstep of the Zhuyang Hotel.

'Hello, welcome, my friend – you are tired, come inside!' shouted an exuberant Peter Xuehu, the chubby, middle-aged proprietor. The bus roared off, and I stumbled inside as if disembarking from a week at sea. 'So, long trip, eh?' Peter Xuehu asked in good, if thickly accented English. 'Go upstairs to dorm at end of hall, take shower, pay me later!'

I found the room, dropped my backpack, and reached for my money belt, only to feel the skinny slickness of my waist. With a sickening, heart-dropping horror, I suddenly realised that it was still tied to the overhead rack of the bus. No! I whirled about in a sudden panic and took quick stock of the predicament. Was this possible? I ripped open my backpack, as if I had put it there and forgotten – not there. What was in it? All my money, my passport, my plane ticket onward from Hong Kong, even my little Nikon One-Touch camera. Impossible! Defying all appeals to common sense, I had stashed every dollar, yuan, travellers cheque and credit card in the belt, with nary a penny in reserve elsewhere. Waves of incredulity and fear rolled over me. I slapped myself and clasped my temples, like the figure in Munch's painting *The Scream*. I checked everything one more time – and ran back downstairs in a panic.

Peter Xuehu was just settling into his easy chair in front of the reception TV, nonchalantly sipping tea from a jar, when this wild-eyed American burst upon him and disturbed his peace. 'What a fool,' he surely must have thought when I grabbed his arm and blurted out, 'The bus! I left my money belt on the bus!' Well, never mind what he thought, I was desperate.

Quick as a flash, he leapt up, grabbed me by the arm and pulled me outside. 'Come with me!' he shouted, almost gleefully, as if this was all in a day's work, and we ran down the street together to a dim shopfront that seemed to sell dry goods and cigarettes.

Peter muttered something to a group of people smoking and playing cards on the pavement, and out of nowhere somebody produced a mobile phone. Peter punched numbers feverishly, while one of his cronies shouted into a walkie-talkie.

'Come, come!' he yelled to me again, and we ran back to the hotel, disappearing together behind a curtain to a rear garage area decorated only with a ping-pong table.

Another several minutes of blasted nerves ensued as I paced vigorously back and forth, while Peter Xuehu kept dialling numbers on the mobile phone, over and over and over until finally the person he was trying to reach picked up at the other end. I had to trust that he was doing what he could for me, without pressing too hard about what was going on.

Finally, lo and behold, a Nissan Pathfinder four-wheel drive pulled up. Peter shoved me into the back seat, jumped in after me, slammed the door, and off we stormed at 110 kilometres per hour across an expanse of bumpy road. I was a travelling man once again, only this time the anxiety was tweaked up to a far higher notch than just an hour before – and I had thought I'd reached my destination.

'Bus end in Guilin,' Peter Xuehu explained finally, 'so we go Guilin! I call to bus station, bus wait for us. Bus go slow, we go fast. We catch bus! But you very lucky if we find money belt. Cannot trust people here!'

Words of encouragement indeed, and I could do nothing but agonise through the 45-minute drive, and marvel that these kind people, whom I had met only a few moments before, should be providing this sort of help. I quickly compiled a mental list of what I would do if I didn't get my stuff back: with no passport, I would have to first get to a US embassy or consulate, in Beijing, I suppose – 2000 kilometres away, or maybe there was one back in Guangzhou. But how? With no money, I'd have to either make fast friends or else look forward to a lengthy hitchhike. Would American Express produce one of those life-saving moments they advertise, and send a guy all the way here to replace my card and travellers cheques? Losing my camera would be bad enough, though that was just the icing on the cake. And who the heck were these people, and how could I thank them?

Finally, we rolled into Guilin and pulled into the darkened bus station. Everything looked dead; it was now after 10 pm, well after Chinese buses quit for the night. I flopped out of the Pathfinder all wobbly kneed, wishing this would just be over, running around in circles, certain my bus was long gone. Then I spied a familiar bus in the corner with its lights on. I ran over, wild-eyed and breathless, and recognised the drivers.

'Oh! Oh!' they grinned, recognising me and laughing. They had arrived only a few minutes before us, and were casually sweeping out the mounds of nutshells and popsicle sticks and cigarette butts from the journey. One of them slowly reached behind the driver's seat . . . and pulled out my precious cargo, all in one miraculous piece. My anxieties literally dropped from my face, as a soothing breeze suddenly drifted across the flat stretch of concrete.

I unzipped the money belt: unbelievable but true, everything was there, just as I had left it. I practically started kow-towing, offering grateful rounds of thanks along with packets of Marlboros.

Peter Xuehu joked with the drivers, smiling and slowly shaking his head. 'You very lucky,' he said to me. 'You very, very lucky.'

Three spies in a diamond tub

Suzanne Possehl

Born and raised in the wilds of New York and schooled in Boston, Suzanne ditched her first and only nine to five job (as an editor for a CIA-funded think tank in Washington DC) and moved to Russia in 1991 to study literature at Leningrad State University. Bread lines, protests and the overall chaos soon lured her out of the library and onto the street. She began reporting for several newspapers and magazines, including the *New York Times* and *US News & World Report*. Fluent in Russian and with a Russian-stitched rucksack, she travelled through much of the Soviet bloc, including three crossings of Siberia, the latest as co-author for Lonely Planet's second edition of *Russia, Ukraine & Belarus*. Once the dust from the collapse of communism settled, Suzanne moved back to New York with her Russian-born husband, Georgi Shablovsky, a photographer and biologist. They now live in Montreal, Canada, where Suzanne teaches at McGill University.

ADRIFT on a pine-green ocean. No mountains, no rivers, just the rim of the horizon and the blue eye of a frozen lake peering upwards and asking why anyone would come this far. Below, a single dirt road cuts into the thick taiga. The pilot follows it north as if he were afraid of getting lost.

For two months, I have been moving further and further away from civilisation. The thought of hotels with electricity and hot water has become a distant dream. I've discovered that a packet of instant coffee in a bottle of mineral water produces a foamy drink – Gulag cappuccino.

I wouldn't mind one now, as this rickety AN-24 plunks down in Mirny, the most northern, desolate Siberian city on my marathon itinerary and, thank God, the penultimate destination before I return home. By now – and this probably happens to any traveller who spends more than a week in Russia's Outback – I have had too much vodka and am starting to hallucinate. I see steamy shower stalls, bubbling bathtubs filled to the rim, even my own chipped tub in Montreal with seashells collected from many shores and pet cacti, the only life form able to survive my extended absences.

Moonish-grey, industrial and crater-like, Mirny strikes me as a setting for a Soviet episode of *Star Trek*. On the airport's doorstep there's a gaping, kilometre-wide diamond mine, spiralling downward like an inverted volcano. The rectangular, ten-storey apartment buildings, snapped together from the same Lego set, sit on stilts above the permafrost. In the middle of the city square, on a granite chopping block, is a metre-high head of Lenin.

This fifty-year-old city, in the centre of one of the world's richest diamond deposits, was once the Soviet Union's most tightly held secret. It's one of those few corners of the world that has been completely unexplored by outsiders. In my mind, that makes Mirny a must-do.

But not before I shed some of this Trans-Siberian grime. Taking my key from a smiling, squeaky-clean hotel administrator behind a well-lit desk, I dash up three flights to my room, dump my rucksack on the nicely tiled bathroom floor and open the hot water tap.

In Siberia, the more strategically important the city was in the good ol' Soviet days, the greater the chances there'll be either hot water or electricity now. Mirny, I quickly discover, has both, but what's coming out of the cold tap is also a scalding, bath-defying sixty-five degrees Celsius! Shuddering to think just how incredibly hugger-mugger this place must have been, I get dressed again, grab my notebook and go out.

The second-largest city in the Yakutia Republic, Mirny (population 39,000) is neat and orderly, a paradise in the tundra compared to the other Siberian cities I've just visited. Despite its monotone veneer, the city has lots of Things to See & Do. There's the market bursting its winterised bubble with Kirgiz melons, New Zealand kiwis and Korean sandals. The city has two diamond museums, complete with mock-ups of the nearby diamond-ore processing factories and plastic facsimiles of the world's largest *almazy*, some of them fist-sized and pulled from the nearby pits.

Being one of two guests in the museum that afternoon, I ask the guide lots of questions. She answers gratefully and glances at the other visitor, a quiet, stocky man with dark hair and brown eyes, who came in about the same time I did and is now following me out.

'Quite interesting,' I offer.

'Where are you going next?' he asks.

Good question, and I ask for his advice. Since I've come all this way, I want more than mock-ups and plastic fakes. Serozha introduces himself and suggests that we walk over to the headquarters of the company in charge of diamond mining and processing. It's another boring Lego building. Serozha stays outside while I go inside in the hope of finding someone who'll arrange a touchy-feely tour of the diamond facilities.

The armed guard immediately directs me to the chief of company security (usually an ex-KGBer who jumped the sinking Soviet ship). Expecting a bear with gold teeth, I'm surprised to be greeted by a 35-year-old in khakis and a buttoned-down oxford. He's got tousled blond hair and wears gold-rimmed spectacles.

'May I help you?' he asks, setting down his cellphone.

I take out my Lonely Planet guide to Russia and slide it across the highly polished, carved Italian desk. He thumbs through.

'Mirny isn't in the book. I would like to add it,' I begin my well-practised spiel in Russian. 'Have you considered that tourism might be good for the city?'

'What do you want to see?' he asks.

'Everything.'

He nods and picks up his phone. The usual procedure would be for me to wait an hour today, a couple more hours tomorrow, all to find out that my request to visit anything – a mink farm, a vodka factory, a caviar cannery – has been denied. But three minutes later we are in a chauffeured car cutting through the city.

From the outside, the diamond-sorting factory is unmarked and looks just like all the other buildings. We pass through triple doors, a metal detector. Alex warns me to be careful handling the diamonds or I could be strip-searched and given an enema on the way out. Apparently real desperadoes swallow them.

We pass a glum-faced English professor in the waiting room, but Alex won't let me talk to him. He whisks me down a pure white corridor and into a room where women in lab coats are sitting behind microscopes. There are cameras in the corner of the room and I suspect there are hidden ones as well. Before I can say Liz Taylor, Alex plops a diamond as big as a bear liver into my sweating palm. Personally, I don't crave precious gems, but the very real possibility that one of these could vanish in my presence is making me nervous.

'We found this last week,' he says, tossing 150 carats in the air. 'It's worth about a million dollars. So are these diamonds.' He hands me a tray of multi-hued, various shaped, gumball-sized rocks.

Then he explains the elaborate security system, the coding, the wax stamps. This is one of those rare moments when you get what you came for. Here's Alex – charming, Western-mannered, no doubt an ex-spy catcher, now with a high-paying job in private industry – and me, citizen of the former enemy state. We're fondling diamonds, laughing, trading stories about the days when the presence of an American in a place such as this would have triggered an international crisis. Everything is changing, and I'm right there, experiencing it all. Seventy years of Siberian secrecy is thawing underfoot.

We go back to the waiting room. The professor is gone, and Alex is pulling a paper and pen from his briefcase.

'So what else do you need?'

Carte blanche, I say to myself, feeling the god of travel is with me. He sketches a plan. Today I see the diamond factory; tomorrow we go down into the mines. The next day I head north, above the Arctic Circle, to visit Anabar, Udachny, places I never dreamed I'd be able to write about. This is a coup d'état for Lonely Planet, I think as we part.

Back at the hotel, the administrator says cheerfully that the problem with the cold water has been resolved, but before I can race upstairs, she adds that a short man with brown hair has been looking for me.

'Him?' I ask, spotting Serozha.

'Hi, how's it going?'

'A great day,' I answer.

'What did you do?'

The question strikes me as odd. As inquisitive as Russians can be, they're usually not this nosy.

'You saw the diamonds. And now you're heading to Anabar?'

For a moment, I just stand there, stunned. Perhaps if this Serozha wore a spangled scarf around his head and lots of gold rings, I might be persuaded of his supernatural powers. But he is just a stocky Siberian with a military wristwatch.

'I wouldn't advise you to go,' he adds softly.

'Why not?'

He shrugs his shoulders and walks away.

That evening, after catching some of Mirny's nightlife (beer and grilled fish in a parking-lot café), I am primed for that long-awaited bath. The water, warm and plentiful, gushes out of the tap. Soon I'm up to my neck in seventh heaven with every dusty village, screaming babushka and psycho-drunk encountered on this trip now far far away. But then there's knocking in the distance, at someone else's door. The floor attendant is saying, 'She's in.'

Now the knocking is louder. I scramble out of the tub and reach for a towel. It's the size of a bath mat. My clothes on the floor are drenched.

'Hold on,' I shout, pulling on last week's outfit from my backpack and opening the door.

Into the room steps a middle-aged Russian in a short-sleeved shirt, unbuttoned to reveal that his chest has a lot more hair than his head. He says something about being from the police department and asks if the blonde girl with him can sit down.

I clear the chair for her, sit down on the bed and try to pat my hair dry with the pillow case. The next thing I know, I am being asked to sign what in Russian is called a *protokol*. It's basically an admission of guilt, only I haven't been told what I'm guilty of. I could ask, but I have a gut feeling that what I really need to do is not argue and get this bare-chested drunkard out of my room as quickly as possible.

'I can't sign,' I blurt. 'I don't have the legal right.'

He bats his bloodshot eyes for a second, then, breathing vodka into my face, says, 'But I thought you Americans were so free!'

'You've been misinformed,' I quickly answer. 'It's you here in Russia who really are free.'

This pleases him. We begin to talk about his city, which I tell him is truly remarkable, one of the best I've been to. Then, I ask for his name. This is probably a mistake. He remembers the *protokol*.

'No, really, I'm not allowed to sign it.'

'OK,' he answers. 'Then I'll just take your passport.'

I shake my head. 'You can't have it. It's US government property.'

In a way I feel sorry for him. He is drunk and just trying to do his job.

'Look,' I say. 'You go home. I'll come by the police station in the morning.'

As I close the door behind him, I can see onto the square outside, where another balding head, this one of Lenin, is bathed in moonlight.

If I were in any other city, I would pack my rucksack and leave. But I am in the middle of the tundra, more than 5000 kilometres from Moscow. One phone call to security at Mirny's two-gate, four-flights-a-day airport and the police could block my only means of escape. I have no choice but to show at the station.

The next morning at sunbreak, I am downstairs calling the operator for Alex's telephone number. I proceed to wake up every Alex Almazov in Mirny. Unbelievably, there are eight of them.

After listening in for a bit, the hotel administrator perks up. 'You're looking for Alexander Sergeevich?' she asks, referring to him by his patronymic. 'His room is the one under yours.'

I do not dwell on this odd coincidence as I race up the stairs and begin pounding on his door. Sleepy, in pyjamas and with his glasses atilt on his nose, he listens to the story of my nocturnal visitor.

'Drunk, without a uniform, in the middle of the night! Uncalled for! You must make a complaint.'

In beautiful bureaucratese he pens off a flowing missive about police misconduct and tells me to sign it.

Taking the pen, I ask nervously. 'Did you recently move to Mirny?'

'Yes, why?'

'Because you're staying in the hotel.' I don't think I have to remind him that not so long ago it was standard KGB procedure to put agents in hotels, next to the people they were spying on.

'Oh, the company hasn't found me an apartment yet,' he answers, yawning.

'You write like a lawyer. Were you one before you came here?'

I admit it's a silly question but I'm desperate to know more about this guy.

He laughs and tells me he went to school in Moscow at the State Institute for International Relations. I'm suspicious: this is an elite school where diplomats are trained for espionage and spies for diplomacy.

'Do you know that guy Serozha who has been following me around?'

'Serozha! You mean that pipsqueak with the greasy brown hair? He's only a KGB major.'

'Only?' I think to myself.

'And that's another thing to put in the complaint. A tourist coming to Mirny shouldn't be trailed by the KGB. It's absurd!'

A sickly chill runs through me as Alex appends the letter.

'I would take this complaint to the mayor. He is responsible for keeping the organs of power in line. He will call the police chief, and when you go over to the station all will be fine. Both that cop and Serozha are going to be reprimanded for this!'

The city administration is opposite the hotel. Crossing the square, I can't help thinking that too many people are becoming involved. All I'm trying to do is add a page or two to a travel guide. That shouldn't require the participation of the police, the KGB and now the mayor.

As I pass the silvery head of decapitated Lenin, I wonder who – if anyone – is in charge here. The mayor is out of town. I meet with his legal adviser, whose eyes become as big as shot glasses as he reads the complaint.

'Everything will be fine,' he repeats.

His hand is shaking as he pulls out an elegant pen and an album commemorating Mirny's fiftieth anniversary. Scrawling his best wishes for my visit to the 'City of Peace' (for this is what Mirny means in Russian), he presents me with the book and sees me out.

'You know, in the old days, Mirny was probably the most secure place in Russia. Because of the diamonds, our local KGB saw spies under every unturned rock. You would have been arrested before you'd even left the plane. But that's all over now. We're glad you're here.'

Then, he adds, 'Make sure that you take Alex with you when you go over to the station. Just in case.'

I ask for his business card. 'Will you be at this number for the next hour, *just in case?*'

'Yes, yes,' he answers, shutting the door behind me.

I walk the two blocks to Alex's office feeling that this is quickly turning into a Kafkaesque game of monkey in the middle, with Mirny's comrades tossing around my dwindling hope to write up their diamond city and be on my way.

Alex, showered, shaved, behind his desk and wielding his cellphone, calls out, 'Suzannochka, what are you doing here?'

'The mayor wasn't in.'

'He wasn't?'

'But I talked to his legal assistant and he says that you should go with me to the station.'

Alex babbles something into the phone and puts it down. 'That's silly. Here, Yuri will go with you.' He points to a hulking man who could do justice to the nickname Scarface.

Scarface grunts.

'See you later. We're set to go down the mines at noon, so make sure you're ready,' Alex calls after us.

Scarface and I get in the back of a windowless van. As we bounce along in the dark, I begin to think that living so far north has taken its toll on these people. They are behaving like characters out of a plot from Dostoevsky, who incidentally was exiled not far from here, in a town named after another nineteenth-century writer and trouble-maker, Chernyshevsky.

Yuri slides the door open and we scramble out of the van. The police yard is walled in, with a row of blue police cars parked in the lot and a wooden building that looks like a fire trap. Yuri shakes hands with the men we pass; it's as if they are congratulating each other on a live catch.

At exactly 9 am, I am escorted into a closet-sized room. Cramped behind a wooden school desk is a large woman wearing a far too-tight uniform. Looking meaner than the drunken cop in my room last night, she is waiting for me with another *protokol*, this one affirming that I hadn't signed the first. It's pretty clear that someone has ordered her to get my signature no matter what.

I have no idea why my signing anything is so important to them, but sensing that my wobbly Hancock will put me on the fast track to the Gulag, I refuse to sign this paper too.

'Get the witnesses in here,' she screeches.

In shuffle two Russian 'witnesses'; one doesn't look eighteen and the other is a flighty woman in her thirties who, seeing I am a foreigner and completely clueless as to what is happening, gives me her address and cheerfully invites me to her home, in Chernyshevsky.

The preliminary interrogation begins. The woman officer accuses me of arriving in Mirny three days ago (which isn't true), refusing to show the hotel administrator my passport (the administrator never asked), disguising my identity as a foreigner (to whom she does not specify) and not having Mirny written on my visa. The last point is true, but I remind her that by Russian law a tourist no longer needs to have every city listed.

'This is Yakutia,' she snaps.

'As far as I'm aware, Yakutia is a republic of Russia, thus, according to the Russian Constitution . . .'

'Hah!! What Constitution!?' she sneers.

I have a similar card to play. I pretend the Mirny police station doesn't exist. As I turn to go, I hear her say to the officers on duty, 'Don't let her leave!'

Now I start to panic. Not having much to lose, I walk out of the room, fully expecting my way to be barred by Yuri's long arm. No-one follows me.

I soon realise that making a run for it would be asking for more trouble. Besides, even if I got out of here, I'd still have to get past security to board the plane.

I slip into a quiet, second-floor office at the front of the building, where a plain-clothed woman sits at her desk.

Calmly as possible, I ask, 'Do you mind if I close the door and use the phone?'

'Go right ahead,' she says.

Alex's line is busy. I dig out the legal assistant's card. His secretary says he cannot come to the phone. Taking a deep breath, I say softly, 'Look, I'm at the police station. They won't let me go. They are trying to arrest me.'

'Oh my God!' she yells. 'Why didn't you say so?! I'll get him. Hold on.'

Instantly, the legal assistant is on the line. 'What's wrong?'

'The police are accusing me of entering the republic illegally, without a proper visa.'

'The police chief . . .'

'He's not in.'

There's a moment of silence, and I can hear footsteps pounding the worn floorboards in the hall.

'What's Alex doing?'

'I don't know. He didn't come.'

'I told you . . . Where are you right now?'

'Hiding in some lady's office.'

'Stay there. Someone will be right over.'

I hang up and thank the woman, who pretends she hasn't heard a thing. My situation is helpless. I'm seven time zones away from the US Embassy. The telephone, needless to say, is blocked for long-distance calls. They could lock me up, and a long couple of weeks could pass before anyone at home realised.

Perched by the window and clinging to my last few minutes of freedom, I page through my notebook and cross out any incriminating evidence: the description of the fun I had a few weeks ago on the black-sand beaches of Kamchatka, skinny-dipping in the frigid Pacific in full view of the border guard's high-powered binoculars; the afternoon I persuaded a high-ranking military man to give me a tour of the missile installations on Sakhalin. I have taken a lot of risks to see, to do, to write. Maybe coming to Mirny was one too many.

I should have known something was wrong the moment hot water gushed out of the faucet. A man chummies up to me in the museum. He turns out to be KGB. I go with Alex to see the diamonds; he grants me carte blanche. That night a drunken policeman barges into my room waving a *protokol*. For help, I go to the mayor. The mayor's assistant sends me to the police chief. The police chief is not in, and some crazed policewoman detains me. Now I'm watching out the window for 'someone'. Who will this be – Lenin with his head sewn back on?

Just as I'm beginning to regret the day I ever applied for a passport, I hear tyres squealing in the dirt below as a car pulls up. Doors fly open. In seconds, I hear voices in the stairwell. A door shuts, and all is silent again.

I come out of hiding. Scarface Yuri is standing in front of the door. He was probably there the whole time. I ask him what's going on.

'They're meeting with the police chief.'

'I thought the police chief was out of town.'

'He came back,' Yuri murmurs, nodding towards the office in which my fate is being decided.

The door is thickly padded. As I'm trying to eavesdrop, it opens. I'm ushered into a room with a large colour television in one corner. A basketball game is on with the volume turned off. A heavily jowled man with thin, whitish hair is giving orders to the police chief. Before I can sit down, he turns and starts firing questions at me. Though he doesn't use the word *spionka*, it is obvious he wants to think he has caught one.

'You just showed up here. By some devious route. You've been in Kamchatka, Sakhalin Island, Vladivostok – all highly sensitive areas. You have no papers, no permission. Why did you come here? Who sent you?'

I tell him I write for Lonely Planet; he looks at me like I am from another planet.

The police chief, who is sitting behind a large desk with a good view of the television, begins reading aloud from a document. Thinking it is about time I ask someone to contact the insurance company that's supposed to rescue LP writers from these tricky situations, I try to interrupt him. His voice drones on. I turn to watch the game but my heart is doing rebounds.

'So,' the police chief says, finally looking up at me. 'By presidential decree . . .'

He means Nikolaev, the President of Yakutia.

My only rebuttal – that having more about Yakutia in our guide might be good for the republic – seems a little lame. I glance over at Alex. How he got here, I don't know, but the whole time he has been silent, turning paler and paler.

I'm beginning to fathom the next six or so months in a permafrost jail cell when the telephone rings. It's a special sort of ring, a frenzied succession of rapid bells that usually means the call is from out of town.

The police chief grabs the receiver. He listens intently, then puts down the phone and screams at the wall for a car. I have no idea what is happening except now the jowled KGB boss is swearing and Alex is shutting his briefcase.

The police chief stands. His mouth is moving, but the words I'm hearing just don't jive with the sentence I'm expecting him to pronounce. What he's saying is, 'I'm sorry.'

Nodding in the direction of the KGB boss, he requests that I depart from Yakutia immediately. This I readily agree to. There is a flight to Moscow in two hours, and I can already see myself on it.

There are a couple questions I would like to ask, but not wanting to sound like I'm arguing with their decision to exile me *out* of Siberia, I thank the police chief and sprint down the stairs.

In the parking lot, Alex catches up to me. 'So what do you say, shall we go down the mine?'

I look at him. He's got to be kidding.

'Or maybe you've had enough for one day?' he asks plaintively, his glasses smudged.

'Enough,' I answer, taking a big gulp of air. All this time I've felt like I was being held underwater. Nothing makes any sense, and I'm rapidly losing hope that there is one clear, logical explanation.

On our way to the airport Alex apologetically tries to explain. 'You know, if you hadn't said you were writing a travel guide . . . Nobody here could believe that! Even *I* thought it was a lousy cover – I mean, what tourist would come to Mirny? Next time, say you are a professor. We get a lot of those.'

Travel in India — the hard way

Mark Honan

After a university degree in philosophy opened up a glittering career as an office clerk, Mark decided that there was more to life than form-filling and data entry. He set off on a two-year trip round the world, armed with a backpack and an intent to sell travel stories and pictures upon his return. Astonishingly, this barely formed plan succeeded and Mark has since contributed regularly to magazine travel pages. He has worked for Lonely Planet since 1991, writing guides to Austria, Vienna and Switzerland, and contributing to guides to India, Central America, Mexico, the Solomon Islands, and Western and Central Europe.

I spent much of the wearisome London–Frankfurt–Mumbai flight fine-tuning my research plans for the *India* guidebook. Anything to take my mind off the pitifully inadequate airline seat. This was not my first visit to India, a rewarding yet challenging country, so I had a good idea of what to expect. I was looking forward to it; little did I know that I was about to endure the worst two days of travel I've yet experienced.

My first task upon arriving bleary-eyed at 2 am was to acquire some rupees. The current *India* edition detailed many hassles, and the lengthy, bureaucratic process of changing money was one of them. When this seemed straightforward at the State Bank of India in the airport, I changed a lot. Too much. I ended up with a brick-sized chunk of 216 hundred-rupee notes. The grin on the face of the bank clerk as he pushed them over told me that I wasn't the first person to make such an error.

Pockets stuffed with wads of banknotes, and feeling extremely vulnerable, I pondered my next move. The first of my research territories was the state of Gujarat, my first port of call Daman, some 150 kilometres north of Mumbai. Because of my tight schedule I had to forgo a hotel stop in Mumbai and press straight on to Daman. But how? Hanging around Mumbai's Central terminus for several hours awaiting a (perhaps non-existent) train, trying to keep awake and guard my bags, was unlikely to be a very pleasurable experience. I decided to quell my backpacker's sensibilities (which dictate one spends as little money as possible in any given situation) and hire a car for the trip. I could sleep on the way, I reasoned, and arrive fresh and relaxed, ready to begin my day's work.

In India, there's generally somebody around who can supply pretty much whatever you want, and sure enough, as soon as I left the terminal building I was surrounded by a hubbub of touts trying to sell me anything from an overpriced stay in a hotel to a selection of illicit drugs. One of their number was a Sikh who offered me a car.

'How much to Daman?' I asked.

'Two thousand rupees.'

'I'll pay 1500 rupees.'

'It will cost at least 1750 rupees.'

'I'll pay only 1500 rupees,' I insisted, and eventually he agreed to the price.

The Sikh told me to wait, and off he went to fetch his car – at least, that's what I assumed. In due course he returned and led me to a small Mumbai taxi, wherein a driver was already waiting. A bit small for such a trip, I thought, but supposed it would do. I clambered in with my luggage, and off we went into the darkness.

A few minutes later we pulled up in a ramshackle side street and the driver told me to get out.

'Why?' I asked. 'You're supposed to be taking me to Daman.'

'I am not licensed for such a trip. You will go in that car.'

I looked suspiciously at the indicated vehicle, a largish, white jeep. Three men approached and loomed over our taxi. I was acutely aware that I was completely at their mercy. I no longer knew where I was, and nobody knew I was here in this deserted side street in the middle of the night; furthermore, my pockets were stashed full of cash. I was going to get mugged on my first night and would have to return to England, defeated and humiliated. Provided I wasn't murdered!

'We will take you to Daman,' one of the men told me. 'Please pay 2000 rupees in advance.'

'I already agreed a fee of 1500 rupees,' I stated feebly, knowing that everybody realised my bargaining position was now severely weakened.

'Fifteen hundred rupees is not possible. Two thousand rupees.'

'Well, take me into Mumbai instead. I'll take the train.'

They weren't having that either, and we finally agreed on a fee of 1700 rupees, with 700 rupees upfront. I took my bags over to the white jeep, grateful that I appeared to be going to Daman after all. The jeep driver, who had been catnapping in the front seat, was prodded awake and we set off. Thankfully, the others stayed behind, and I was finally able to relax a little.

I looked at my watch and saw that it was now 4 am. I estimated that 150 kilometres should take about three hours – perhaps less, as the roads ought to be fairly empty at night. I should be there for an early breakfast, I predicted, as I arranged my backpack into a serviceable pillow and lay down on the back seat.

I managed to doze a little during the first hour or so, even though we stopped and started a great deal. The car would surge forwards for a few seconds then sharply cut back to idling speed, nearly throwing me off my seat. Then we would speed up again, only for the same thing to happen. While this was going on, the vehicle would also veer sharply one way then another. In my semiconscious state, I decided that the driver must be dodging potholes in the road, and tried to think no more about it.

At about 6 am, as darkness was gradually giving way to pre-dawn grey, my curiosity got the better of me and I sat up to see what was going on. A dismal sight greeted me. Although this was the main traffic artery up the west coast, it was by no means a multi-lane highway. The road was fully jammed in both directions with nose-to-tail trucks – lumbering, fume-belching monsters with nothing moving much faster than walking speed.

The reason for our frequent changes of speed and veering progress soon became apparent. Not content to sit calmly in such slow-moving traffic, my driver would seize on the slightest gap to try to overtake the vehicle in front. Unfortunately, this was not achieved in a cautious or measured manner – quite the contrary. Sometimes he would even swerve dangerously in front of oncoming vehicles and attempt (with little success) to drive along the unpaved hard shoulder on the wrong side of the road. Such rash manoeuvres were especially worrying as visibility was very poor. It was raining and a sheen of grey dust covered the wiperless window.

To take my mind off imminent disaster, I pulled out my travel atlas and tried to work out exactly where we were. I was dismayed to discover that we had covered barely a third of the trip. I thought regretfully of the blissfully untroubled train ride that I could have taken instead: being whisked smoothly across the landscape in air-conditioned comfort and safety, in about half the time and for about a tenth of the cost. Other visions crowded into my mind; I pictured with unsettling clarity the near-fatal road accident suffered by a researcher while working on the previous edition of *India* – the very researcher who had warned me in a pre-trip email that 'Indian roads are suicidal'.

My mood wasn't helped by the numerous truck carcasses piled along the side of the road. Some had apparently been there a while, but others had obviously been incapacitated only very recently, in the last day or two. The metal was newly crumpled, and once or twice I saw the driver and his companion sitting idly by the wreckage, presumably wondering what they should do next. Sometimes the cab section of the truck was horribly mangled, and there was no doubt that the unfortunate driver had failed to survive the impact. But not all of the immobile trucks had been in accidents – many had simply broken down. Some were still in the middle of the road, creating additional traffic chaos.

To pass the time, and to try to distract myself from such depressing sights, I read what the guidebook had to say about this road, Highway 8. 'It's the major route for trucks travelling between Mumbai and Ahmedabad', I learnt. Furthermore, the road 'would have to be one of the most congested in India, so expect delays'. No need to change that comment, then. Leafing further through the book I came across an unsettling article entitled 'Road Safety'. It began: 'In India there are 155 road deaths daily – an astonishing total'. The piece continued: 'Most accidents are caused by trucks, for on Indian roads might is right and trucks are the biggest, heaviest and mightiest'. And then: 'Day and night there are crazy truck drivers to contend with'. Enough already!

Many of the trucks I saw were eye-catching. They had signs declaring 'All India Permit' or specifying the particular states they were allowed to traverse. They bore evocative manufacturer names such as Ashok Leyland or Tata. The cabs were often colourfully painted and had strings of beads or statuettes of Hindu gods hanging from the windscreen or mirror. Then again, some cabs were in a terrible state – no windscreen, no rear-view mirror, not even a driver's door. The sight of religious accoutrements adorning the trucks was not as comforting as might be supposed. A common belief amongst drivers was that road accidents were not caused by carelessness but were the result of pre-destined karma – this explained a lot about local driving habits!

During moments of complete gridlock, some drivers would leave their stationary cabs and walk round their vehicles, kicking the tyres, checking their load or even making minor repairs. A fight broke out on my left; two drivers were throwing punches and tugging each other down to the ground. Several other men were quickly converging onto the scene, one bearing a dangerous-looking wooden club.

By now I felt more than a little unhappy, and was seriously concerned that I wouldn't survive the trip. I sat bolt upright in the middle of the back seat, luggage placed on either side to form a semblance of a barrier between me and the chaos outside. My every muscle was tensed in anticipation of a horrendous impact.

As much as I wanted to think about anything except this road journey, I couldn't stop myself studying my driver's every move, and flinching with each risky manoeuvre. As soon as the opposite stretch of road was clear he would immediately veer out to over-take the line of trucks ahead. When vehicles on the other side approached us, he would continue to hog the centre of the road until the last possible moment, often forcing the oncoming traffic to change course. Conversely, when oncoming traffic was over-taking, he would hold his line on our side of the road, even if able to yield some space. It was a stupid, dangerous macho game of 'chicken', and it certainly made me want to lay an egg or two.

As the trip continued, my driver became increasingly agitated, excited and erratic. If any of the oncoming vehicles had the nerve to pull exactly the same sorts of stunts he himself was pulling, he would bash his horn, thump the steering wheel, direct torrents of Hindi abuse at the culprit and even sometimes feint towards them as if to instigate a collision. This despite the fact that he was usu-ally facing off against a massive truck, and there was no question who would come off worse if there was an impact!

At 9.30 am, after almost six hours on the road and with my nerves in tatters, we finally reached the turn-off for Daman. I directed the driver to Seaface Road, where most of the hotels were clustered. I thrust the agreed fee into the driver's hands and started gathering my bags.

The driver took the money, counted it, and shot me a reproachful glance. 'My tip? *Baksheesh*?' he queried.

Here's a tip, my mind shouted – find another career in which you're not going to kill someone. This trip took twice as long as I expected, cost more than I wanted, and scared me more than I could possibly have imagined. A tip? I don't think so. What I actually said was less eloquent than that, but I think he got the message.

I checked into a nearby hotel. At this stage, any normal traveller would have exhaled a huge sigh of relief, ordered breakfast, watched a bit of TV, and settled down for a long snooze. But not me – I had a job to do, and I couldn't afford to fritter away even one day. I showered and went out to start my research.

Daman proved to be an uneventful little coastal town that survived on fishing and alcohol. An ex-Portuguese colony, it was now administered as a union territory, which meant that alcohol consumption was permitted, unlike in the surrounding Gujarat territory. As visiting Gujaratis couldn't take it with them, they stayed put to imbibe large quantities of intoxicating liquor in numerous high-street bars. This did plenty to contribute to the local economy, but had less beneficial effects on the balance sheets (and indeed the sense of balance) of the visiting Gujaratis themselves.

By midday the following day my research was duly completed, and it was time to move on. My next stop would be Surat, a busy, industrial town ninety kilometres to the north. There was no question I was going to take the train this time, so I squeezed into a shared taxi with seven co-passengers for the ten-kilometre, thirty-minute trip to the nearest railway station. I joined the scrum of Indians clustered around the ticket windows and eventually emerged with an unreserved second-class ticket. Unfortunately, a reserved seat was not possible – I would have to take my chances along with everybody else.

I waited alongside families with huge packing cases of luggage, young men with bristling black moustaches and coal-dark eyes, and old men with white stubble and bowed legs. There were children extending grubby hands for donations of small change, platform vendors dispensing tea and small snacks, and (as often in India) the odd cow snuffling for edible morsels within the drifts of garbage.

About forty minutes later the train chugged into the station. My heart sank. The rear of the train, the part with the unreserved second-class carriages, was already jammed full, with dozens of people hanging out of the open doorways. The train rumbled to a halt and very few people squeezed out of the congestion; about ten times that number attempted to force their way in. By some accident of fate, I found myself at the front of the press of people, who all propelled me, pack strapped to my back and day pack strapped to my front, towards the carriage. In the melee someone swung a suitcase overhead and into the doorway. It caught me a glancing blow on the side of my glasses, which spun off my face. Somehow I caught them before they hit the ground and were smashed underfoot.

What happens when an immovable object meets an irresistible force? Who knows, but in this case the implacable opposition of the crushed people within the carriage didn't quite match the intense effort of the people trying to board, and ever so slowly, centimetre by centimetre, I found myself being squeezed inside the train. Most people didn't make it – quite a few didn't even try; the task was well beyond the elderly, young and infirm. I suppose I had been lucky.

Pretty soon I wished I hadn't been. It was impossible to move. People were even standing on the edges of my sandals; if I'd attempted to lift my feet from the floor, the soles would have been ripped from the uppers. Every time anybody around me tried to move their feet, I was kicked in the ankle or had my toes stamped on.

Although my feet couldn't move, my body was gradually being pushed further into the carriage by the people hanging out of the doorway who were trying to win a less dangerous vantage point. I was soon about ten degrees off balance, supported by the crush of surrounding bodies. I scrabbled my fingers against a smooth-sided wall, vainly trying to gain enough purchase to achieve a better equilibrium.

Then people started yanking at my backpack, which was taking up valuable space. There was no way I could manipulate my arms to get it off, and nowhere to put it anyway. But the yanking continued, and it soon escalated into pushing and shoving. Threatening phrases in Gujarati were shouted into my face. My glasses were once again knocked off my face; the right eyeglass popped out of the frame, and I was fortunate enough to catch it before it was lost forever. Somehow, the combined efforts of a dozen pair of hands managed to lift the backpack off my back and place it in my arms. There was still nowhere to put it, but I simply let it go and it stayed where it was, supported by who knew what bits of bodies beneath and around it.

Now all there was to do was wait, stare vacantly and semi-focused though my broken glasses, and hope I didn't pass out in the fetid, heavy atmosphere. The open doorway yielded a tiny amount of fresh air but there was a lamentable lack of activity from the ceiling fans. Sweat started trickling down my torso, and I experienced the disturbing certainty that much of it must have emanated from neighbouring bodies pressed against me.

Most Indian trains are not built for speed, and the kilometres trundled past agonisingly slowly. They also stop frequently, and resume their journey only after an irritatingly long interval. At every stop a few people fought their way on and off, resulting in a new round of jostling for position. Need the toilet? Forget it – there was no chance of reaching one. Similarly, no ticket collector came around, as circulating through the carriage was impossible. At one point somebody or something somewhere beneath my backpack started pinching and pushing at my knees and shins. I was concerned that a child was being crushed under there, but it proved to be a middle-aged man desperately trying to win himself enough space to stand up.

Finally, joyfully, after two and a half hours of slow torture, Surat hove into view, heralded by a grimy skyline of belching industrial smokestacks. Never had such ugliness been so welcome. I battled my way to the door and surged out of the train like a cork from a champagne bottle, almost toppling over as I leapt the surprisingly long distance down to the platform.

I walked shakily out of the station, negotiated a ridiculously noisy and chaotic traffic junction, and checked into the nearest decent hotel.

'The train was incredibly crowded,' I informed the receptionist wearily. 'Is it always like that?'

'Ah,' he said, 'this is Diwali, our New Year festival. Everybody is on the move at this time. Everyone wants to visit their family.'

I gulped. 'Does that mean I won't be able to get a train reservation to Vadodara tomorrow?'

'I am most afraid that there is no chance. I have already tried for another guest without success. The only possibility of getting on a train at all is to take the 5 am service which originates at Surat.'

This was not what I wanted to hear. But yet again, my tight schedule did not allow me to rest up in Surat for an extra day. Somehow I mustered the energy that evening to research a few hotels and restaurants, find something to eat, and get myself tucked up in bed before midnight.

Unfortunately, another surprise awaited me. One thing Indians particularly like to do over Diwali is let off fireworks. My hotel room overlooked the bus station where thousands of people were milling around. It looked (and sounded) as if half of them were letting off firecrackers and rockets. The glass in my window reverberated with each loud detonation. Many people were camped out, apparently waiting for morning buses, so it seemed certain the fireworks would continue all night.

Happy New Year, I thought morosely as yet another firework cracked like thunder right outside my window. Some welcome to India – two horrendous journeys and two nights without sleep. Surely it can't get worse.

Thankfully, it didn't.

Lost in Madagascar

Matt Fletcher

After leaving art college with a degree in ceramics, Matt traded a damp flat in England for camp sites under African skies. The northern coast of Mozambique and the Maralal International Camel Derby provided inspiration for a writing career which started at *Outdoors Illustrated*. Now a freelancer, Matt's travel and trekking articles have appeared in a wide range of newspapers and magazines. When not in distant mountains or down at the pub, Matt plays football, tries to improve his languages and sleeps.

MADAGASCAR, a place where 'adventure travel' could easily describe a taxi journey across town. A place where things are done differently.

This realisation hit me as soon as I arrived at the swirling chaos of Ivato International Airport, where smiling hustlers, money changers and taxi drivers mixed with customs officials, immigration officials and incoming passengers. The gentle anarchy of Madagascar will either fill your heart with joy or leave you with a nervous twitch that requires two weeks in a darkened room to overcome.

It was March when I arrived. My fellow passengers included a diminutive old man, who carried a Scottish terrier in a hold-all; hundreds of over-laden returning Malagasy, who begged other passengers to carry on a piece of their hand luggage; and a handful of eco-tourists, the great hope of Madagascar's woeful economy. It's the amazing weirdness and diversity of the country's fauna and flora that attracts eco-tourists. Much of the wildlife is endemic, a consequence of the island's 160 million years of isolation when its unique plants and animals had the place to themselves, happily evolving until man (probably arriving from Indonesia and Malaysia) gate-crashed the party and began to screw things up some 2000 years ago. The wildlife that remains, some of the most amazing in the world, is showcased in a network of national parks, Madagascar's trump tourist cards.

I was in the country looking for some of the aces, on assignment for an adventure travel magazine. I'd planned a five-day trek along the freshwater Pangalanes Canal, which stretches some 650 kilometres down the east coast from the major port of Toamasina. Often separated from the sea by only a few hundred metres, the canal links a network of beautiful lakes in its northern section and is lined by huge swathes of littoral forest. I wanted to walk through this dense and humid rainforest before widespread logging and slash-and-burn agriculture reduced the whole lot to a charcoal-littered sandpit. But first I had the urban jungle of Antananarivo (Tana for short) to contend with.

Tana is one of the world's shabbier capitals. It's predominantly low-rise, poor and in an advanced stage of post-colonial decay. The French-style boulevards may be wide and airy, but rubbish is piled high and broken sewers lie in wait for the unwary traveller. After a while, however, the city develops a certain gritty charm, and for one reason or another I spent some considerable time there. It may not be a pleasant sight in the rainy season or smell too sweet at the height of summer, but the flood plain surrounding the city is beautiful after the rains and the downtown area around the Zoma market has a vibrant (if a little seedy) street life. Behind its grubby façade the city is full of interest and intrigue. Spend any time in the bars and restaurants of Tana and your head will fill with stories of dodgy logging concessions, mysterious airstrips cut into the heart of the rainforest, sapphire mining and gold smuggling on a grand scale. It's also the best place to organise adventure travel excursions.

Our trekking party consisted of three locals and three 'tourists' – myself and two travel agents. Nancy was from Paris and Nivo was from Tana. We spoke French, though by the end of the first day shrugs and strained expressions were the common language. Vivi was our English-speaking guide, entertainer and source of intelligent information about the forest and the country. He had a radiant face that let everyone who came into contact with him know what a happy, friendly and contented kind of guy he was. People were his strong point, and though he wasn't a guide in the truest sense of the word, he was the perfect person to look after hapless tourists. But Maminty and Nary were the ones who really led the way. Both were strong and incredibly lean, managing to glide effortlessly through the forest while the rest of us struggled constantly with the undergrowth. Maminty, his face as wrinkled as elephant hide, played the old and wise character whilst Nary, his young apprentice, got to carry the daily provisions and all the heavy gear. Maminty carried a short pole with what looked like a machete attached to the end of it, which as time wore on and the vegetation grew thicker he used rather a lot.

Getting lost was not supposed to be on the agenda. Ours was a well-organised trip, more organised, in fact, than I initially realised. We were transferred from Tana by four-wheel drive and speed boat, and each night a support crew would sail on ahead to a pre-arranged spot, set up camp and wait to feed us. Cool drinks were always on hand for the weary travellers and we even had a packed lunch each day (which Nary carried). Although I had brought my usual camping and trekking gear, I might as well have left it all in England. On this trip I was going to get spoilt, which was rather a novel experience, and as we drove out of the Central Highlands surrounding Tana I relaxed and stared out of the window dreamily, content to people-watch all the way to the east coast.

On the first night we established a base camp beside a wide section of canal south of Ambila-Lemaitso and drank (too many) cold beers sitting on the shore of the Indian Ocean. I remember thinking that the sky that evening was the most amazing I'd ever seen and fell asleep to the sound of a million romantic frogs and endless crashing waves.

We had breakfast at first light and caught a lift up the canal to the trailhead at Ambila-Lemaitso. According to Vivi, the village was once hailed as 'Madagascar's San Tropez', filled with fun-seeking French officials, managers and service people posted thousands of miles from the French Riviera. Now only the Hôtel Relais Malaky, with its neglected tennis court, remained to remind Ambila-Lemaitso's handful of visitors of a different age. A railway line still ran through the village, which had a station of sorts, but the timetable might as well have been written in invisible ink. Once I heard the sound of a train drifting through the forest, but I never saw one.

Across the river from the Relais Malaky, past the collapsed bridge and abandoned (and never used) World Bank-sponsored river port, a trail ran into the forest. It was wide enough for a four-wheel drive and looked well used. For a good half-hour I was lulled into thinking that all the trails in the forest were going to be as easy to walk, but sure enough the track soon narrowed. Away from the village and lands cleared for cultivation the landscape alternated between open scrubland, secondary degraded forest and primary littoral forest. Walking through the primary forest was the most comfortable, despite the immediate rise in humidity that made the sweat sting my eyes. I was thankful for the protection the vast canopy provided against the sun, which shone with such force it caused Nancy's unprotected face to swell up like a balloon.

Every now and then the land dipped down into thigh-deep swamps surrounded by traveller's palms, the symbol of Madagascar. Within the hollow stems of these fan-like trees was a reservoir of cool, clean drinking water, and Maminty showed us how to tap them successfully. Occasionally we'd catch a glimpse of the grand canal, completed thanks to much Malagasy labour in 1904 and opened with great fanfare. Today only the first 450 kilometres are navigable, but the northernmost section remains alive with pirogues (dugout canoes) and taxi-boats ferrying goods, people and produce to and from Toamasina.

We walked on into late morning, and Vivi kept a steady stream of information coming, frequently pointing out such natural wonders as the crab spider, the fast-disappearing 'for the ants' snake (which burrows into ant's nests, becomes too fat to leave the burrow, and is then eaten by the ants), tree frogs, edible fruit and medicinal plants too numerous to name.

'Does Anita Roddick know that around 65% of all endemic Malagasy plants have medicinal properties?' I asked him jokingly.

'Who?' Vivi replied, though when I explained he told me that many foreign universities and research teams certainly did know this and had made a habit of coming over, studying them and returning home to patent their DNA.

By midday the trail had become a confused and overgrown animal track with a habit of disappearing. Frequent bouts of bitching and cursing from Maminty signalled that things were becoming even worse. The words spoken, half in jest, by Vivi as we had driven out of Tana began to weigh heavily on my mind. 'We will be the first people to walk this route in six years.' As the people and clapperboard houses had flashed by I'd thought nothing of it, but I was now beginning to realise the importance of his words. We were going to get lost in the jungle.

Things had certainly changed since the last trekkers had walked this way. Three major cyclones had torn through since then, and the last one (in January 1997) had killed more than 100 people and left around 30,000 homeless. These meteorological upheavals, along with more than half a decade's forest growth, had altered the trails somewhat, so that when we finally hit the shore of the Pangalanes Canal Maminty gave thanks (or at least that's what Vivi told me he said). We had a celebratory lunch before swimming in the cool clear water. Refreshed, we set off again and immediately picked up what was thought to be THE trail. Two hours later we were totally lost and had begun to cross and re-cross swamps, back-tracking, cutting fresh trails and getting absolutely nowhere.

After hours of this behaviour you had to look on the bright side. At least I was getting to see the forest at close quarters, stumbling upon treasures such as a beehive of sweet wild honey, which Nary tried to harvest, much to his cost; pitcher plants next to a lake inhabited by Nile crocodiles; and an amazingly beautiful horned chamcleon we must have walked past twice (such is the benefit of backtracking) before Vivi spotted it. Lemurs (cute, furry and dim-witted mammalian ancestors of monkeys and humans) are one of Madagascar's greatest tourist draws and Vivi assured us repeatedly that he had often seen brown lemurs in the area. Every flash of light through the canopy or moving shadow suggested that a whole troop was about to come swinging through the trees.

By late afternoon there were obviously diverging opinions amongst the guiding staff, who were talking with increasing haste and expression in Malagasy, whilst casting furtive glances in our direction. This was not a good sign. It was getting late and endless walking was getting us nowhere. All the decent drinking water was gone (we were onto brown swamp water with a couple of Puritabs thrown in for luck) and above the sound of the frogs calling to each other across the swamp was the relentless drone of mosquitoes.

In a last-ditch attempt to get to the evening's camp we found the canal's overgrown fringes in the gathering gloom and followed the waterway north, wading barefoot through the very bilharzia breeding grounds my doctor had warned me about. After fifteen minutes squelching through God-knows-what, my head filled with thoughts of burrowing parasites, it became clear that we weren't going to make it before nightfall. We were defeated. All we could do was make a rough camp beside the canal, light a dirty great fire, get Vivi to tell a few stories and sit it out. In reality we were in no danger, and as the stars lit up the sky and a gentle breeze picked up, bringing the roar of the Indian Ocean drifting across the canal, being lost in the rainforest didn't seem too bad a way of spending an evening after all. Eventually someone would see our fire and come to our rescue. Wouldn't they?

And so they did, just as I had resigned myself to a case of malaria and an early-morning swim through crocodile-infested waters, and Vivi was winding up the story of how Maminty had ended up owning a bed that belonged to the first president of Madagascar. The hero of the hour was Francis, manager of the Bushhouse Hotel where our trek was to end. We had been missed and he was the cavalry, spotting the burning branches we'd started waving as soon as we'd heard an outboard motor. We sped the frustratingly short distance to our camp site by the light of the full moon and were treated to cool beer and wonderful Malagasy stew.

The next few days were almost as adventurous. Where there was no other way through, we waded across waist-deep mangrove swamps and caught pirogues across the deepest of channels. Every now and then Maminty was forced to cut a way through dense vegetation so that we could follow a route he was sure had been there six years before. We eventually made our way to the shore of Lac Ampitabe and on to the village of Ankanin'ny Nofy (the 'House of Dreams') where the luxury of the Bushhouse Hotel awaited.

Tales of Tuscany

Bruce Cameron

Bruce has used a wheelchair since the age of seventeen. In 1993, following seven months holidaying in the UK and Europe, he left his twelve-year-old banking career to write a travel guide for wheelchair-accessible travel in Australia. After facing the usual traumas of funding and finding a publisher (he went it alone in the end), *Easy Access Australia: a travel guide to Australia* was published late in 1995. Bruce contributes to Lonely Planet's guides to Australia, and is busy completing an access guide to Melbourne and building a Web page for *Easy Access Australia*.

TRAVEL for most people is a simple exercise. Decide where to go, book a plane ticket, pack your backpack and you're off. For someone who uses a wheelchair, however, there are a few more difficulties to face. Decisions such as how to travel, where to stay and what to see or do assume monumental proportions. The fear of getting to a destination to find that there's no access to the accommodation because of an insurmountable step or because the doorways are too narrow, and you can't get into the bedroom or worse still the bathroom, is enough to prevent some people from having a holiday at all. It is simply easier to stay at home.

And so it was with a certain amount of anxiety that I decided to accept an invitation to join a friend in the United Kingdom to travel through France and Italy. The first leg of the journey took us to the south of France where we rented a farmhouse. The property was supposed to be wheelchair-accessible but it took several faxes between Melbourne, London and the property owner in France before I was willing to accept it. The fear of getting stranded never completely disappeared.

As our car crunched along the gravel driveway approaching the farmhouse I could feel my anxiety levels rising. I clambered out of the car, breathing deeply to help stay calm, and wheeled my way to the front door. Were there any steps? Was the door wide enough? Once safely inside, I moved towards the bathroom. Were the doors wide enough? Was there sufficient space to manoeuvre into the bathroom? Was there access to the toilet and into the shower? Could I reach the taps and turn them on without getting scalded? Then to the bedroom. Again, was the door wide enough? Was there room to turn around? Was there access to at least one side of the bed? Was the bed high enough so I wouldn't get stuck trying to get off it?

It was only after I'd satisfied myself that I could get to the bathroom and into the bedroom that I could start to relax, unwind and enjoy my holiday.

We enjoyed two weeks of exploring the Périgord Vert in the Dordogne Valley before heading towards Italy. The planning was completed from our farmhouse. After scrutinising dozens of brochures and making many phone calls to London, we booked a villa, La Casina, situated between Florence and Siena. The managers assured us the property would be accessible and even measured door widths for us.

Our journey through the south of France took us to Montpellier and Nice, where we stayed at brand-new Formula 1 hotels with eminently accessible rooms, before arriving at a hotel in Florence, which had been recommended by a very reliable contact in London. Although confident about the standard of accommodation, cultural differences and the language barrier caused deep anxiety to develop as we approached each new hotel, only to dissipate after inspection.

Our stay in Florence was a stunning experience, visiting historic sites such as the Uffizi Gallery, the Duomo and Ponte Vecchio, although I can't recommend bumping around cobblestoned streets in a wheelchair as a recreational activity.

Our departure from Florence was uneventful once we'd figured out the correct exit from the Florentine ring roads. We headed south towards Siena and our turn-off at Poggibonsi, passing through rolling hills neatly cropped with olive groves and vines protected by windbreaks of tall trees. Despite the beauty outside the car, I became aware of an increasing feeling of anxiety within.

The further south we went, the further back in time we seemed to be going. Travelling through an area dotted with medieval villages and ageing peasant farmers wandering along the roadside caused me to doubt the wisdom of our decision to come here. How could these people possibly provide a wheelchair-accessible holiday, in such an apparently ancient land?

We missed our turn-off – it must have been an omen – and it was mid-afternoon before we finally turned onto the road to our villa. 'Road' is not quite the right description: it was a long, narrow, bumpy, pot-holed track which appeared to lead to a dilapidated farmhouse perched precariously on a hill. Fearing the tumbledown structure was our villa, I forced myself to concentrate hard and breathe deeply to maintain a façade of calm. I was a little relieved when I noticed the track ran past the old building towards an olive grove to the side of an adjacent hill. What was to be our accommodation came into view as we rounded the olive grove – a large farm building converted to holiday villas standing on a hill above the olive trees. Constructed of the same sun-bleached, sandy-coloured stone and roofed with the orange clay tiles typical of nearly all the buildings of the region, it looked pleasant indeed.

Our host, and the property's owner, came out to meet us with greetings of *buongiorno*. Introductions were made in appalling accents. Our host was Paolo, a local school teacher with a kind, round, smiling face. He was accompanied by Alvarre, the 'house man' (or maintenance man), a tiny, heavily sun-tanned, almost weather-beaten man. Paolo had limited English, Alvarre had none, and we had no Italian.

Gesticulating for us to we follow, Paolo headed to the front door. My anxiety settled a little as I entered the house over a small bump. The doors opened into a ceramic-tiled, living-cum-sun-room with sofa, table and chairs, with a door to a small kitchen off to the left. Straight ahead was a door to a short passage, which I could see turned left, presumably to the bedrooms and bathroom.

I motioned that I wanted to explore the villa. Approaching the door to the passage, I could tell it was going to be a close shave, but when the 'push rims' hit each side of the doorjamb I panicked. The door was only just too narrow for my chair to fit through. My worst fears had been realised. Where was I going to sleep? On the sofa? And what about the bathroom? Panic turned to anger at myself for becoming stranded, and frustration at realising our translations must have blurred the measurement information. I took a few deep breaths, and tried to think of ways to overcome the predicament.

Perhaps if we removed the push rims I could fit through the door. I conveyed my intention to Paolo, who translated to

Alvarre, who scurried outside, soon to return with a tool kit. As he knelt down and started to loosen the nuts holding the push rims in place, I realised it wasn't going to work: both wheels would have to be dismantled, the tyres deflated and removed.

I indicated that Alvarre should abandon Plan A, and with a comforting hand on my shoulder and what was supposed to be a reassuring smile, he surveyed the offending door. Rapid-fire Italian followed between Alvarre and Paolo, with much gesticulating and waving of hands. With a wink, Alvarre disappeared to return with a hammer, a small crowbar and several large screwdrivers.

While all this was going on I was trying to stay calm, and think of an alternative plan of action. The best I could come up with was to retrace our steps to Florence, but I was exhausted by the driving, the anxiety and the stress.

Meanwhile, Alvarre had begun to remove the door, lifting it from its hinges. Then, to my amazement, he used the crowbar to ease the doorjamb away from its plastered wall. A snow storm of plaster fell onto the tiled floor. My anxiety and annoyance were soon replaced by guilt for being the cause of all this damage as I watched the doorjamb peel away from its secured position.

Alvarre stood back and motioned for me to try the opening. I cautiously moved forward, passing through the widened opening with only a centimetre to spare, until my feet hit the timber-panelled wall opposite. There wasn't enough space to swing left into the passage beyond! My anxiety was turning to despair as I removed my 'footplates', in the hope that it would shorten the turning space needed. It didn't.

More animated Italian ensued, with Paolo finally suggesting we give him an hour or so and promising that things would be fixed upon our return.

We returned two hours later to find Paolo and Alvarre in the cleaning-up stage. While we had been away, Alvarre had removed the entire timber-panelled wall opposite the first door and had prised the second doorjamb away from the wall!

My bedroom at the end of the passage, which had taken us about four stressful hours to traverse, was large, bright and ceramic-tiled, with huge windows and wide views of olive groves across vines to a distant hill and the towers of San Gimignano. The bathroom had also seen Alvarre's screwdriver, the shower screen having been removed to create an easy wheel-in shower.

Paolo, Alvarre and I shook hands as I thanked them profusely. I was able to relax, at last.

Last rites on the Tatshenshini

Jim DuFresne

Jim is a former sports and outdoors editor of the *Juneau Empire*, and is the first Alaskan sportswriter to win a national award from Associated Press. He works as a freelance writer, specialising in outdoor and travel writing. His work for Lonely Planet includes the *Alaska*, *Tramping in New Zealand* and *Hiking in Alaska* guides.

WHEN I was offered a spot in a rafting expedition down the Tatshenshini and Alsek rivers while updating my guidebook, *Alaska: a travel survival kit*, I jumped at the opportunity.

The trip down the two wilderness rivers is often regarded as one of the most spectacular in North America. The rivers form a ten-day, 177-kilometre journey that begins in Canada's Yukon Territory, slices through British Columbia and ends up on the rugged coast of Alaska's Glacier Bay National Park. The landscape is not just beautiful – it's mind-boggling, a blend of towering mountains, immense glaciers and vast expanses of moving water.

The other reason I didn't hesitate in accepting the offer was because I'd once worked for the guiding company that was outfitting the trip. I knew the three guides who would be rowing the rafts and leading a party of nine down the river. One of them, Ed, was a close friend.

I have trekked and paddled throughout Alaska, but this journey would exceed even my high expectations of wilderness adventure. It took me through a slice of the world so pristine that I doubt I'll ever experience such purity again. And it taught me a lesson about life, death and moral obligations that I will surely never forget.

The expedition began in the city of Juneau, where I met Ed in advance of the clients and other guides. Together, we hauled a mountain of equipment onto an Alaska Marine Ferry bound for Haines, loaded up a van and made the first gear run to the remote launch site in the Yukon Territory. Early the next morning, the day of our departure on the river, we made a second run.

Raft expeditions are equipment-intensive. Our inflatable boats were two and a half metres wide and five metres long; they could comfortably carry four to six people and would depart loaded with gear – campstoves, tents, portable tables, boxes of wine, and ice chests full of salmon, fresh vegetables and steaks. Guides sit in the middle and work the oars. They don't propel the raft but row only to position it, allowing the river's swift currents to do the work. Clients sit along the air-filled walls and enjoy the ride past stunning scenery.

It's first-class travel in the wilderness. Rafts can open up some of the most remote areas of the world to people who don't have the skills to paddle a whitewater kayak or the desire to shoulder an eighteen-kilogram backpack for a week. They still have to sleep on the ground at night but happy hours precede a dinner of grilled halibut and a Caesar salad.

At the launch site we met a Canadian biologist who was spending the summer counting salmon. A little later, as we were assembling the rafts, a kayaker stopped by, carrying his small whitewater boat and gear. He quietly studied the river for a minute and then casually asked Ed if he had ever run the Tatshenshini. He wasn't nervous or cocky, just calmly curious of what lay ahead.

Ed described the canyon reached within the first hour of the float, a gorge with steep granite walls and Class IV rapids. It's the most challenging whitewater of the entire ten-day journey and it hits you right at the beginning with monster curls, maddening boils and thunderous drops.

'You're welcome to caravan with us,' Ed offered, but the kayaker politely declined, saying he wanted to depart shortly.

By mid-morning the clients had arrived, the rafts were inflated and loaded, and our party was anxious to get under way. While we donned our rain gear and life vests, Fred, the expedition leader, carefully detailed the run through the canyon and the safety procedures should anyone fall out.

Despite Fred's warnings, none of the clients were ready for the whitewater that came so soon into the trip. One minute they were getting adjusted to sitting on a tube of air, the next they were staring at a two-metre curl that broke across the front of the raft and drenched them with gallons of cold water. For a continuous hour and a half the river boiled, churned and exploded around half-submerged boulders. The guides took on one devilish swirl after another, muscling the rafts away from crashing hydraulics and holes, breaking their concentration long enough to shout at their passengers to lock arms and lean into an approaching wave.

When the Tatshenshini finally calmed we were a wet but joyous group. We pulled out of the river to reorganise and celebrate, slapping hands and hugging each other, agreeing there was no better way to begin a wilderness adventure than surviving such a canyon.

Our euphoria, however, was quickly doused.

We had barely shoved off when we floated past an empty kayak lying upturned on the riverbank. It came into view so quickly that we didn't have time to stop and retrieve it. I'm not sure what the clients were thinking; I suspect they didn't realise its serious implications. But I was alone in the equipment boat with Pete, the third guide, and we immediately looked at each other, stunned.

Within minutes our worse fears were realised. There, lying face up on the riverbank, was the lone kayaker. The first two guides swept past too quickly to land right away, but Pete managed to pull our raft in nearby. We ran along the shore, praying that he was just injured and resting.

When we reached him I immediately turned away. I had never encountered death in the wilderness before. I had never seen a body outside of a casket. The kayaker looked at peace with himself; his eyes were open and his arms were at his side, but right below his helmet was a deep gash in his forehead.

There was no question he was dead.

'We'll haul him back to the equipment boat,' said Fred, having made his way back upriver. He sent somebody to grab a tarp and five of us struggled to carry the wrapped body along the Tatshenshini's rocky bank.

We floated to where we had planned to stop for the day – a wide, moss-covered gravel plain along the river. Our immediate concern was the fact that we had a body in bear country. Brown bears are opportunists. When the salmon are running, they'll catch them. When berries are ripe, they'll pick them. And if there is carrion around, they'll smell it. They'd much rather eat something already dead than spend the energy chasing their dinner.

We wrapped the body tightly in the tarp, carried it almost a kilometre from the tents and strung it up high in the trees like a food bag. Brown bears can't climb trees, and we were hoping there weren't any black bears around.

The next dilemma was what to do.

We had no immediate communication with the outside world. We weren't carrying a portable radio or cellphone, and our emergency signaller was only good if a plane was practically overhead. It could be days before we spotted a bush plane in the area, if at all.

What should we do?

It was clear that some clients, while saddened by the mishap, were worried about their trip. They had forked out more than $1500 for the guided expedition, not to mention airfare from places from as far afield as Colorado. It was safe to say that none of them would ever run the Tatshenshini again, and they were becoming increasingly resentful towards the corpse that might disrupt their long-awaited adventure.

Leave it here, they said. Contact the Canadian Mounties at the end of the trip. Tell them that there's a dead kayaker on the Tatshenshini.

To the guides and myself, this was an unsettling thought. We all craved wilderness adventure, and at one time or another had all gone solo. It wasn't a macho ego that propelled us into the woods alone, or even a desire to test our outdoor skills. It was simply the lack of a paddling or climbing partner, of going solo or not going at all.

Death I could handle. It was the accepted risk you took any time you entered the mountains or floated a river. It was being left out there that bothered me. There was nothing more horrifying to me than the thought of perishing alone and being eaten.

Pete was even more distressed. A skilled climber and paddler, he had soloed often and, although he never said as much, I suspect had faced a number of close calls. Those times when you're trapped high in the mountains by a sudden storm, hunkering behind a boulder, trying to warm half-frozen fingers, wondering how you're going to get back down. When you're fording a swollen river and halfway across you realise the current is overpowering you, that if you lift a boot, you'll be swept downstream.

Moments alone when for a split second you think, 'If I die, please take me home.'

Dinner was sombre and the few discussions we had were serious. A decision had to be made, and Fred, as the head guide, had to make it. When he finally revealed his plan it came as no surprise to me. He had no intention of leaving the body out here, and he certainly wasn't going to take it along with us.

Fred announced that he and Pete would depart early the next morning and bushwhack on foot the fifteen to twenty-five kilometres we'd floated the first day. Without the aid of trails or even an accurate map, they would follow the banks of the river and return to the launch site, where they knew the salmon-counting biologist had a radio. The rest of us would take an unscheduled day off on only the second day of our trip.

'What if you don't make it in a day?' someone asked. 'What if you need a couple of days to reach the site?'

Pete shot an angry glance that could clearly be seen in the glow of the campfire. What if we do?

By the time the clients were up the next morning Fred and Pete had been gone for almost two hours. Idle minds were not a good thing, so after breakfast Ed organised a hike into the surrounding hills. When only half of the clients elected to join him, he deputised me as 'assistant guide' and asked me to stay put with the rest of the party.

Then he handed me a short-barrelled shotgun.

'What's this for?' I asked.

'There's a body in the trees. Remember?'

'Oh. So if a bear comes into camp, I'm suppose to shoot it, right?'

For the first time in twenty-four hours, Ed smiled. 'It makes the clients feel better when they see a gun. Just don't tell them you've never used one before.'

I spent the day sitting around, flashing the shotgun to nervous clients once in a while but mostly pondering – over and over again – my one close call while soloing.

By 10 pm we had finished dinner, and had begun to discuss where Fred and Pete might be and the possibility of spending another spare day with the kayaker.

Some thirty minutes later, when the conversation had slowed to a crawl, Ed and I suddenly looked up at each other. Somewhere in the distance we could hear a very faint hum.

If you spend enough time in the Alaskan wilderness, waiting at enough remote lakes, river bars or glaciers for a bush plane or helicopter, you eventually develop an ear for the hum of their propellers. The more trips you take, the better you get at distinguishing the whirl of a propeller from the natural sounds that have been serenading you for a week – even if it is still miles away.

Five minutes later a helicopter was hovering over our camp, looking for a place to land. We all ran to it and watched as Fred, Pete and a Canadian Mountie emerged. After the body was retrieved and the police departed, we broke into our supply of boxed wine for the first time that trip.

We all felt tremendous relief; our conscience had been cleansed. Suddenly we were in a state of euphoria that was sweeter than when we had survived the canyon.

At some point in that evening of celebration we acknowledged the kayaker, honouring him with a toast and reflecting that he had died doing what he probably loved best. We could now be at peace with ourselves for the next nine days, knowing he'd received his last rites on the Tatshenshini and was heading home.

Postscript: We later learned that the victim was an experienced whitewater kayaker named Paul from the town of Burnaby, British Columbia. The cause of death was listed as heart failure.

The motorcycle diaries

Nick Ray

A Londoner of sorts, Nick studied history and politics at the University of Warwick, a course which gave him a taste for strange happenings in strange places. Dabbling in journalism for a time, he soon realised that the grind of the tube and the nine-to-five bind just weren't for him. He wound up in Cambodia quite a few years ago and just can't seem to keep away. These days he considers Cambodia a base of sorts, although his work in Africa and Europe makes it a pretty vague definition of 'base'.

NICK Ray has spent far too much time driving around Cambodia on his not-so-trusty Honda Baja while putting together a new edition of *Cambodia*. This short selection of mishaps and misadventures on the road shows something of the perils of relying on an ill-maintained and old motorbike in remote areas when carrying no spares and knowing nothing about the most basic repairs, including where the oil goes. To make matters worse, he has no licence back home so is officially not even able to drive a slowped.

Phnom Penh and the art of motorcycle maintenance

'I think we are going to be robbed,' I muttered to my entertainments coordinator, Chris.

'Yeah, I think we're going to be robbed,' he mumbled back.

It didn't seem much of a big deal after a marathon tequila and marijuana session down at the Heart of Darkness, but then the Heart has a special way of leaving you not really caring about much apart from old Jam songs and whether to brave the barndance brothel that is Martinis or the techno palace of Manhattan. We'd settled for home, as it was supposed to be one of those 'quiet nights' that just never quite happen in Cambodia, but we got more action than we'd bargained for thanks to a *moto* driver who had an uncanny aversion to driving faster than twenty kilometres per hour. Try and do the right thing by leaving the bike at home when you are out on a large one and things will inevitably go Pat Pong on you.

Crawling down Monivong Boulevard at snail's pace, we might as well have carried a megaphone requesting people to rob us. I could sense motorbikes starting their engines on dark corners of Phnom Penh's leading commercial strip, ready to pounce at any moment. Call it the ganja fear, but I had a bad feeling about the ride. We hung a right at the Ministry of Tourism on 232 Street, and after a few junctions it became apparent we were being followed and that our *moto* man was no Barry Sheene when it came to quick getaways. A bike pulled alongside and the guys started shouting in Khmer, which seemed to be our signal to fall off the *moto* and have a large handgun pointed in the general direction of our heads. It was something out of a movie, and we were too baked to take it very seriously. We raised our hands and stared at the stars, me thinking, 'I should have had another tequila,' and Chris thinking, 'I don't know if I can hold my arms up much longer, they're too heavy.' And no doubt deep down in our subconscious, untainted by the noxious weed, we both thought, 'I want my Mum.'

They felt around our pockets liberally, so liberally in fact that I began to fear we might become victims of molestation rather than robbery. Chris had a massive 500 riel in his pocket – that's about fifteen cents in total – and I had a whopping $10, which I'd just borrowed in case we changed our course and hit a nightclub. I hoped they wouldn't club us out of spite, for we hardly represented rich pickings. Instead, they added credence to my theories of molestation by pulling off my fleecy jacket. This pissed me off more than the money or the inconvenience of being held up at gunpoint, as Phnom Penh was in the middle of its coldest snap in years. And then it was over before we knew it, probably only a minute in all, but in the freeze-frame action of a stoned mind it seemed like an eternity.

We scrabbled around on the ground in the vain hope that they might have left some of our personal effects, but no, they had taken the lot, including my Visa card – although I've no idea what it was doing in my wallet in a country with no ATMs. We walked around the corner to the guesthouse and saw a few friends lurking outside the gate.

'You won't believe it!' we yelled. 'We've been robbed!'

'So have we!' was the response. It turned out they'd lost a lot more than us paupers, including passports, cameras and watches.

Unbelievably most of our stuff was later found near the guesthouse, neatly stowed in a plastic bag, including the passports, the Visa card and other forms of ID. Robbers with a conscience! But what didn't come back was my coat – I had been well and truly fleeced.

A genuine booze cruise

It was a big game, not just any old football match, but one of the clashes of the year. After the disappointments of France 98, I was putting my faith in the finest talent of the English Premier League to keep me entertained. It was an FA Cup clash to savour, bringing together the teams that have shaped English football during the last two decades – Manchester United and Liverpool. I was anticipating some serious entertainment with the likes of Michael Owen and Dwight Yorke on the same pitch.

First though I had to get to a TV, straightforward enough these days in Cambodia, but it had to have satellite. I had spent the day at Kamping Poy, a vast dam constructed by the Khmer Rouge during their years in power, intended to fuel their vast irrigation schemes that would carry Cambodian rice production to new highs. It was about thirty-five kilometres from Battambang, Cambodia's second city, sophisticated enough for its hotel rooms to have TVs. Some hotels also provided a pretty fruity adult channel on Zero that left little to the imagination. This could be quite a temptation for a young man with a remote control to hand, especially during half-time.

It had taken me almost two hours to get to Kamping Poy, so I figured it would take about the same to get back. But I hadn't figured on my own stupidity, which was to cost me several more hours. I was motoring along, musing over which team I wanted to win, when the bike began spluttering, usually a sign that the petrol was running low. A few more shudders nearly sent me tumbling over the handlebars, and then the engine died on me. I confidently reached down to flick my fuel switch on to reserve, only to find to my annoyance that it was already there. I cautiously eased open the petrol cap, hoping to hear the tiniest of sloshes that might take me further. *Ot mien, nada,* nothing – it was completely empty. I wasn't going anywhere until I got some more fuel. There were very few people on the road, most Khmers being wary of bandits and robbers and returning home from their Sunday picnicking early. Worse still there were none of the ubiquitous Fanta and Johnnie Walker bottles full of petrol sitting on the side of the road.

105

I started to push the bike in the direction of Battambang, vainly hoping that there might be a petrol seller just around the corner. But no, somehow I had managed to run out of fuel on just about the only road in Cambodia that didn't have petrol for sale every ten metres. Just as I was beginning to wonder if I was going to miss the match, I came upon a roadside shack, which sold basic foodstuffs, soft drinks and alcohol. My first thought was to buy a bottle of Wrestler muscle wine and forget about everything; my second was perhaps more stupid still – to buy a bottle of Royal Whisky and bang it in the petrol tank.

As I parted with my riel, the Khmers stared at me, unsure what was going to happen next. It obviously wasn't often that a sweating, ranting, white-faced alcoholic passed by their way. They thought I was going to neck the bottle, and to be honest the thought did cross my mind, but I restrained myself and gestured at the petrol tank. The look of collective horror said it all. '*Ot lahore, ot lahore,*' they shrieked. 'No good, no good.' I figured it was my only chance to catch the match of the year, so in it sloshed, 750 ml of Cambodia's finest whisky, which isn't very fine at the best of times, but particularly not when running a motorbike engine.

Naturally, it didn't start the first time, nor the second; it was perhaps the twenty-third, when my patience was about to snap. The Khmers thought it was the daftest thing they had ever witnessed, but I'd remembered the stories of America's Great Depression when cars were run on moonshine. It may not be as cheap an option as petrol, particularly if you run out of petrol in Scotland or Saudi Arabia, but in a crisis it will get you home.

Incidentally, Liverpool led 1–0 for the duration of the game, only to be overturned by two late goals which gave Man U a 2–1 victory.

The legend of the Beast

I first heard rumours of the Beast when I was chewing over a pizza on the riverfront in Phnom Penh. It was a 'happy pizza' – pizza à la ganga, if you like – and I was in such a state that I knew

I just had to find the Beast. 'Breakdance' Baldwin, the man who had taught the Khmers a thing or two about windmills and swan dives at their New Year celebrations, had come across it the week before: 'It's shit, man. It's the worst motorbike you've ever seen, a Ssangyong 125 from another century.' Its home was Ratanakiri, Cambodia's Wild East, and my friend Andrew and I were heading up there to find out if there were any trees left after the logging, any animals left after the poaching or any American soldiers left after the fighting, lauding it Colonel Kurtz-style over the local hilltribes who inhabit the province.

Days later we tracked the Beast down to a small restaurant in the dusty provincial capital of Banlung, and indeed it did look like it was manufactured around the time of the Penny Farthing. Five bucks later and I was heading out on it along yet another of Cambodia's evil roads, one with potholes that eat Cambodians for breakfast.

We were flying along, the Beast straining to hit fifty kilometres an hour at max revs, when a loud bang went off nearby. Extremely nearby in fact, as it was the back tyre blowing out. The bike went disco on me, nearly putting me face down in the shale. Finally pulling the Beast to a stop, I got off to inspect the damage. It was a serious blow-out and half the inner tube was in tatters. We were literally in the middle of nowhere, Bokheo twenty klicks east and Banlung twenty klicks west, neither of which exactly qualified as civilisation in any case. All we appeared to have to look forward to was a slow roast in the sun, Andrew's only observation being: 'I'm dark about this, it's really ordinary.' We had no water and I was already feeling the madness of dehydration clawing at my skull.

It's fair to say that madness did overcome me after a few more minutes under the grill. I decided to cut out the inner tube. Quite how this was supposed to help the situation, I still don't know, but the small crowd of locals thought it was pretty funny. Enough was enough; I was likely to start frothing at the mouth if I stood there any longer, so I figured I'd just ride on the rim.

'*Ot te, ot te, ot te,*' the assembled crowd of Khmers cried out in unison, 'No, no, no,' and rushed over to grab the bike. Oh great,

I thought, now they are going to take us to their village and make us drink ten litres of rice wine, normally something we'd be more than up for but not when we were already raving. But no, instead they made a coordinated swoop for our *kramas* (scarves) and began earnestly stuffing them into the deflated tyre. I couldn't quite believe they were serious, but yes they wanted me to ride back on cotton rather than air.

Somewhat incredulous, I eased out the clutch and the bike began to move. It was a precarious ride into town, as the back wheel had a mind of its own, which seemed to be in a permanent state of disagreement with the front. I was swinging around like a waltzer at the fair, and on more than one occasion went very close to licking the road, but I somehow wobbled my way into town.

I took the Beast back to its owner, Miss Naeh, who took one look at it and said, 'Nick, bike very sick.' She had a point, but it wasn't half as sick as me after spending all day in the sun – the *kramas* didn't look too pretty either after spending an afternoon in a tyre.

Life on the edge

We'd heard that Bou Sraa in Mondulkiri Province was one of the largest waterfalls in Cambodia. We'd also heard rumours that the road out there was the bastard child of the devil himself. We were barely halfway down the 37-kilometre road before we were able to confirm the second of the rumours, but we had to drive through at least two major rivers before we could confirm the first.

A marathon two hours later, we emerged at what looked like a pretty major waterfall. To get anything to eat we had to once again take on a river, this time wider and faster and with a fairly ugly drop. I set off across and, after a few ice-rink incidents on the slimy rocks, wheel-spinned my way out of trouble onto the other bank. Next in the river was Simon, and his 'Aaah, no problem' attitude didn't last five seconds as the bike took a completely different course from him and ended up stalled and underwater. The prospects of everyone getting across safely looked slim, so I suggested they waited for me on the safe side while I steamed on to Pinchinda for noodles or rice or whatever else they might have in the village at the ends of the earth.

As I jumped around the kitchen in a small tribal hut, throwing powders in the noodle pan, I began to think we might get a decent meal out of the day. The owner of the house didn't seem too flustered by having me in her kitchen, and her neighbours soon joined in the fun. I pulled away having met half the town, with a sturdy bag of noodles tied to my handlebars.

Back at the waterfall, the rest of the gang had disappeared. I eased my bike into the water ready to cross, and feeling confident took the direct route across the top of the falls – something I soon came to regret. A short distance across, I was poised to wobble through the fast-flowing current. I eased up the throttle and the front of the bike simply vanished from under me. I felt myself falling to the right in the direction of the waterfall and the tasty current seemed to have designs on me. Clinging to the bike seemed the only sensible option, as it weighed an absolute ton. So cling I did until I could pull myself up to a standing position and swing around to the other side of the bike. I felt around the tyre and realised I'd dropped into a sinkhole. Pulling hard on the handlebars, I yanked the thing backwards and upwards, all the while making sure I had a buffer between myself and the thirty-metre drop.

I finally hauled the thing out after more than fifteen minutes of sweating and swearing. I crawled over to the edge of the falls to set eyes on two naked white boys wading into the splashpool. 'Bastards!' I shouted. 'I've come off.' They eventually made it up to 'rescue' me, and I learned to my horror that they had met a Cambodian family of picnickers and had been tucking into ginger chicken and cold lager for the best part of half an hour. I'd risked life and limb to bring them what now appeared to be little more than a mess of river water and skinny worms, while they had been dining in style with ales to wash it down.

Afterthoughts

If you are heading to Cambodia and fancy taking on the country's surly roads with a rented motorcycle, there are a few more evils you may have to face. 'Lucky Lucky New New Thieving Thieving All Kinds of Motorcycles' might well rent you a motorbike one day, only to steal it from you the next. Then there are the notorious traffic cops of Phnom Penh. They'll pull you up for anything, including driving with headlights during the day, although they don't seem to have a problem with Khmers travelling without headlights by night. And last but not least you don't want to have an accident in the country. The best scenario is you'll end up paying for the damages whether you are responsible or not. The worst is something that happened to a mad German guy by the name of Amadeus. One week he was a devout Buddhist on a mission to help Cambodia. After a high-speed crash, a long time out cold on the tarmac with a dislocated shoulder while being relieved of $300 cash by helpful locals, he was losing his religion. He was last seen drunk, bruised and bandaged in Siem Reap, wiggling his trigger finger up and down in the air, shouting: 'I vill kill zem all, I vill kill zem all. You see, zis finger still works.'

Falling for Greece

Rosemary Hall

Rosemary was born in Sunderland, England. She graduated in fine art, but fame and fortune as an artist eluded her, so she spent a few months bumming around Europe and India. After teaching in northern England, she decided to find somewhere more exotic, finally landing a job in Iraq. Now living in London, Rosemary has contributed to Lonely Planet's guides to Iraq and Greece.

I planned to catch the daily bus from Argostoli to Fiscardo, on the Ionian island of Keffallonia. My packs were ready to grab after a lunchtime kebab at my favourite taverna, my reward for working twenty-four hours a day – well, not quite, but as I'd now started dreaming about my work updating the Lonely Planet *Greece* guide, it just seemed that way.

On my way to lunch I spotted some apartments that looked promising candidates for inclusion in the guide. Three tourists sunbathing in the garden confirmed that their accommodation was wonderful, but the whereabouts of their landlord, Dimitreos, was unknown.

Eventually I tracked him down at the local *kafeneio*. When would I learn that if a Greek guy wasn't at work or at home, chances were he'd be in the *kafeneio*? According to the Lonely Planet guide, a *kafeneio* is a café-cum-pub, 'the last bastion of male chauvinism in Europe where Greek men while away their time'.

At my request for information Dimitreos began psyching himself for a leisurely chat over a drink, but I had work to do.

'*Seega, seega,*' he advised – 'slowly, slowly' – a popular Greek saying that's anathema to me when I'm in LP researcher mode.

'I'm catching the two o'clock bus to Fiscardo,' I said.

'Stay another day,' he suggested.

'No, I have a tight schedule,' I insisted.

But Dimitreos's *seega, seega* approach increased, as my time, patience and eager anticipation of a mouth-watering kebab dwindled.

Eventually we embarked on a snail-paced tour of his wonderful apartments, and then, finally, like a bat out of hell – well, as far as this was possible shouldering two heavy packs – I was bus station bound. Trouble was, in a country where serendipity rules,

113

and ferries are often days late, buses are not only punctual, but often leave early.

Halfway to the bus station I spotted a dog lying in the sun. Greek dogs are masters of the 'hang dog' look. It's something I believe they've devised to attract the attention of English tourists, who tend to cosset their pooches as they would delicate children, unlike Greeks who are more inclined to treat them, well, like dogs.

I travel a lot, so can't have an animal companion. Well, nothing requiring more tender loving care than, say, a stick insect, a creature which even in someone as soppy about animals as me fails to evoke an 'Aaah.' Consequently, I indulge anything cute and furry I encounter. Just as I was wondering whether I had time to stroke this dog and say a few affectionate words (for I'm sure dogs the world over understand English), I tripped, and *whoops* (or, more appropriately, my entire vocabulary of obscenities), I was closer to the dog than even I in my yearning to impart affection had intended, and was staring into his eyes, which conveyed, 'How dare you disturb my siesta?'

After the consolatory thought that I could have landed *on* him instead of a hair's breadth *from* him (and a dog's life, even when it's not in England, is surely better than no life at all), I considered my own plight – sandwiched between two packs in a horizontal posture I wouldn't have attempted in an advanced yoga class.

Agonisingly, I scrambled to my feet to assess the cause of my fall – a long strip of metal jutting from the pavement. I momentarily considered suing the bastard who'd put it there, perking up in anticipation of a six-figure sum award. This idea I hastily dismissed, because if I hadn't time to spend an extra day somewhere, how was I going to stick around long enough to fathom the Greek legal system? I needed this delay like I needed a hole in the head, and judging by the blood pouring from my brow I had just that.

Now Keffallonia, unlike London, is not a place where someone lying on the pavement would be ignored. So why did no-one come to my rescue? Because everybody was asleep, of course, for in Greece the siesta is sacrosanct. I've lain in bed all night listening to a cacophony that would awaken the dead, but been accused of an execrable crime for speaking above a whisper during siesta. At any other time my spectacular fall would have been the talk of the neighbourhood.

So, nauseous, dizzy and bleeding copiously, I hobbled into the bus station. On islands, school buses often double as public transport, and approaching the bay for Fiscardo I saw by the masses of children and teenagers that this was one such bus. Quasimodo, the Elephant Man and Frankenstein's monster rolled into one couldn't have caused more of a stir. Shrieking, they recoiled from me in terror. Mind you, I knew all about kids overreacting from my other job (teaching in London), where a bug, only visible to me under a microscope, can cause a fracas and a bee in the classroom evokes mass hysteria.

Despite the bus's no smoking signs, many of the kids lit up, except those older ones who were too busy snogging and the younger ones who were bashing one another over the head with their school bags. Awesome mountain and coastal vistas were ignored until we passed a naturist beach and they became hell-bent on getting an eyeful of the naked tourists, shattering their peace with piercing whistles. All hope I'd had of any recuperative peace had gone out the window, along with empty Coke cans, crisp packets and chocolate wrappers. What was it with these kids? Presumably they'd never had to step over used syringes on communal balconies of tower blocks, or been confined to tiny inner-city flats with violent videos for company; maybe they just had too many doting relatives with whom they had to celebrate all those long and outdated festivals – for the Greek tendency seems to be 'any excuse for a knees up'.

At Fiscardo, I was 'picked up' by the charming Nikos whose mother owned some *domatia* (rooms let to budget travellers). Nikos was the age of many of the kids on the bus, but his ensuing kindness during my stay in his mother's lovely room reinforced my belief that children individually were great, and only became unbearable en masse.

On the way to the *domatia* I told Nikos about my fall. 'You must go to the hospital in Argostoli,' he said, concerned.

'No, I'll be OK,' I said. After the hassle I'd had getting away from Argostoli, neither wild horses nor cute dogs would have dragged me back – I just wanted to sleep.

When I looked in the mirror the next morning I was confronted by the mother of all black eyes, and a lemon-sized bump above it. My fringe covered the bump, but to hide the eye I had to wear sunglasses morning, noon and night. Usually I wore these on top of my head, where, miraculously, they had stayed when I'd fallen. This wasn't just for the image: it also helped me in my work, as seeing through a glass darkly, combined with myopia, meant I might miss something such as promising-looking apartments, cute dogs or even metal strips on pavements.

But wearing my shades had an unexpected bonus. Normally I wouldn't even put the rubbish out without eye make-up on, but now that it was superfluous, not having to apply it (and reapply it, when necessary) saved me ten precious minutes a day.

However, sometimes I just had to reveal my eye. Electricity is expensive in Greece so, understandably, lights are left off whenever possible. When hotel proprietors showed me around their dim, shuttered rooms I'd lift my shades so as not to miss anything. And in that inane way the English have of saying sorry inaptly (such as when someone bumps into them), I'd apologise for my eye, as if the damned thing was my fault – divine retribution for preferring animals to children, perhaps?

In gloomy cafés and shops I also needed to lift my shades. Most people were sympathetic, except for the occasional pissed English tourist who would quip, 'Had an argument with the boyfriend, did you?'

My eye went through all the colours of the rainbow, only returning to normality back home when all my waking hours were spent putting my research onto computer – wearing my eye make-up, of course.

The Mongolian Scramble

Paul Greenway

Paul caught his first tropical disease in 1985, and has had the 'travel bug' ever since. Gratefully plucked from the security and blandness of the Australian Public Service, he is now a full-time traveller and writer. He has written a diverse number of Lonely Planet guides, including *Mongolia*, *Madagascar & Comoros* and *Iran*, and also wrote the Maluku and Irian Jaya chapters for *Indonesia*, and co-wrote the *Middle East* and *Arabian Peninsula*. During the rare times Paul is not travelling, or thinking, reading or writing about it, he watches every minute of every possible Australian Rules Football match, has regressed to his teens and wants to play in a heavy rock band again, and will do anything to avoid settling down.

AS the water rose above my knees, I remembered what I had told my editor when I'd first begun writing for Lonely Planet: 'I will go anywhere.' And here I was, in the back of a jeep, contemplating the unpleasant possibility of drowning in the middle of a raging torrent in a desolate stretch of northern Mongolia.

To avoid a six-hour detour, my driver had decided to drive across the fifty metre-wide river (which hadn't existed two days before, nor was on my map). Predictably, the tiny Russian-made jeep had stalled. Now I was 'supervising' (read: panicking), balancing my money belt, camera and notes on my head as the water rose to my waist – and we hadn't yet reached the halfway point across the river.

The driver and guide swam out of the window and somehow found the crank, which fitted into the lower part of the jeep's engine. In tandem, they took huge gulps of air, ducked under the water, and strenuously turned the crank, thereby forcing the jeep forward about two or three centimetres. Every thirty seconds, they both burst to the surface gasping, took more gulps of air, ducked underwater again and laboriously moved the stubborn jeep another fraction. By the time we reached the middle of the river, the water hadn't risen above my chest, and with everything I treasured balanced precariously on my head still dry, survival seemed a distinct possibility. It took about six hours to cross the remaining forty metres to the other side of the bank.

Later that afternoon, we took the engine apart and laid every piece in the sun to dry, along with everything from my backpack. Suddenly, about fifty horses of varying hue galloped past, skidding down the steep embankment to drink from the flooded river. They whinnied in pure joy and, as the twilight faded, returned single file across the steppe. It was a typically majestic way to finish off a typically frustrating day of travelling around Mongolia.

During my three months' research, I travelled about 15,000 kilometres overland, but rarely faster than thirty kilometres per hour. A jeep is the most efficient way of getting around for visitors, but most Mongolians travel by motorbike, camel, horse and even yak because public transport is so unreliable and so infrequent. An experienced jeep driver is vital, because major roads regularly split into about ten different tracks at the top of a hill – three tracks will disappear into a swamp ninety kilometres in the wrong direction; three others will end up back at the town you've just left; another three will go in circles. Often in consultation with local nomadic families, the driver will find the right track – but not always. We once spent twenty-four hours panicking (well I was; panicking is not a Mongolian trait) as we tried to find the correct track in the middle of the hot, barren Gobi desert. And an interpreter-cum-guide is also very useful because almost no-one outside of the capital city, Ulaan Baatar (UB), knows any English words except 'hello' and 'dollars'.

It could be the warrior-like bloodlines from Chinggis Khaan (known to the West as Genghis Khan), a penchant for wrestling or habits from the communist days when demand always exceeded supply, but Mongolians rarely queue – they bustle, huddle and do the Mongolian Scramble when they buy tickets for a train, and look for precious seats. Buses are also problematic: the vehicles are often Russian rustbuckets, breakdowns are mandatory and drivers are sometimes drunk. On one trip (which left at 8 am), the conductor and several passengers commandeered the bus while the inebriated driver was having a leak by the side of the road. The conductor drove the bus to the next town and telephoned the police, who later arrested the stranded driver.

Very few Mongolians can afford to fly, which is probably a blessing. The major domestic airline is called MIAT, which some wags claim stands for 'Maybe I'll Arrive Today'. MIAT uses aircraft that even Aeroflot has discarded, and the planes often lack toilets, air-conditioning, food or visible safety equipment. Expertise in the Mongolian Scramble is vital to buy a ticket, obtain a boarding card, have your luggage weighed, get to the door leading to the tarmac and find a seat on board (the number of tickets sold often exceeds the available seats). If you arrive safely – and at the correct destination – the Scramble starts again to get off the plane, find your luggage (if it hasn't been diverted to Bolivia or Yemen), plough through the throng of departing passengers and find transport into town.

I often had to take any form of transport I could find. I spent a memorable four days travelling with a great bunch of tour guides and foreign volunteers in a converted East German ambulance to the far west of Mongolia, where foreigners are as rare as, well, yak's teeth. In the provincial capital of Altai, we asked a landlady if many foreigners stayed at her hotel. She thought for a while, then brightly responded: 'We had one once. He didn't stay long. They are rare.' The previous foreigner was possibly the author of the earlier Lonely Planet guide to Mongolia, which goes to show how many foreigners stay in this part of the country.

Travelling independently can sometimes be tricky. The sacred mountain of Shiliin Bogd Uul is apparently close to the disputed, undefined and unfenced Chinese border. After we spent several glorious hours exploring the mountain, our jeep was suddenly followed by a Mongolian army jeep, and then stopped by a stern machine-gun wielding soldier. He leaned into the driver's window, confiscated the keys and asked our reasons for being near the border. We obviously didn't say what he wanted to hear, so he forced us to detour to the military barracks and then questioned us for five hours. I was firstly accused of being a Chinese smuggler, and then, because I don't even remotely look Chinese, of being a Russian spy. The Mongolian soldiers had never heard of Australia, and failed to comprehend my guide who constantly explained that I was 'from a lonely planet'.

The soldiers eventually made several, unhurried telephone calls to some contacts in the tourist industry in UB before they grudgingly accepted that I could actually be a guidebook writer. We then had to drive forty kilometres back to our hotel to collect our bags at about 11 pm – thereby breaking Mongolian Travel Survival Tip No 2: 'Never travel overland in any vehicle at night: if the potholes don't get you, a wandering yak will.'

Mongolian Travel Survival Tip No 1 is 'Always carry a bottle of chilli sauce', because the food in Mongolia is, well, bloody awful; gastronomic purgatory. Almost every meal outside of UB, in a restaurant or home, is a choice of either boiled or fried mutton (ie any slab of dead animal) – and the more fat, the better. Liberal doses of spicy sauce can hide the texture and taste of mutton, and help the lumpy, fatty and hairy bits slide down the throat. The smell and taste of mutton seems to permeate everything. Biscuits, soap and even the local currency smell, and it took several weeks to get rid of the mutton smell from my body after I returned home (where the smell of boiled fatty mutton is not cherished).

If travelling around Mongolia is hard, researching can be a nightmare: banks and bridges collapse overnight; hotels and borders open and close at will; airline, bus and train schedules alter every week; and exchange rates change by the hour. Just before I arrived, there was an outbreak of bubonic plague in the west, and in the north forest fires had destroyed pastures the size of Belgium. Halfway through my research, the communist government fell (after seventy years in power), and a day later the major currency for visitors (the US greenback) was outlawed. By the end of that week, a cholera outbreak had quarantined one-third of the country.

Probably nowhere in the world is the phrase 'forewarned is forearmed' more appropriate than Mongolia. Armed with packets of instant noodles and soups, bottles of chilli sauce and, maybe, a snorkel, I will be well prepared to tackle once more this overwhelming but magical country.

Riding out the big one

Randall Peffer

Randall is a widely published travel writer, with contributions to *National Geographic*, *Smithsonian*, *Islands*, *Travel Holiday* and *Sail*. He is the author of Lonely Planet's travel guide to Puerto Rico and the coordinating author of *Washington, DC & the Capital Region*.

San Juan, Puerto Rico — 19 September 1998, noon

'Hurricane who? Hurricane where?' I find myself sweating these questions in response to a warning from María, an old black lady who runs a popular kiosk on Piñones Beach. My wife Jackie, infant son Jake and I have just cruised up to María's wooden shack to fill our bellies after a morning on the beach. Ten days ago we took an apartment on the island so I could write my travel guide to Puerto Rico. But today I'm not thinking about work; I'm trying to orchestrate the perfect *Fantasy Island* day for my family.

'You'd better get busy, americano,' María chuckles. 'This Hurricane Georges is going to shake things up!'

She cracks open a cold can of Medalla beer and pushes it toward us. But this news of a hurricane has taken the fiesta out of my day. I thank María and tell her we don't need a beer right now. She looks at me, rolls her eyes as if I am refusing mother's milk, and helps herself to the open beer.

'*Viva la isla,*' she chants. Long live Puerto Rico.

'What did she say?' asks Jackie, who does not yet speak the island idiom.

'Readiness is all,' I lie. It is my favourite line from Shakespeare.

19 September, 8 pm

As we push Jake in his stroller down a seaside promenade, Jackie is talking about the brilliance of the stars, but I am hardly listening. I am looking at the royal palms and colonial buildings, but picturing a bomb blast. My mind is writing lists of things we will need to survive the coming apocalypse. When we stop for espresso at an outdoor café, Jackie wonders aloud about the quiet that has settled over the city. The waitress says the *huricán* is coming: everyone except us has gone home to mix up a pitcher of piña coladas, drink up a storm and make love like there's no tomorrow. What else?

'Fill the car with fuel, buy bottled water, stock up on batteries, don't forget Pampers,' I think. I've got a long list of 'what else'.

'We'd better get going,' I say to Jackie.

'Good idea,' says the waitress with a wink.

I get the feeling we're talking about going to very different places.

19 September, 11 pm

As soon as we put Jake to bed, I make three trips to the market. What a bonanza. The store is open, stocked and lifeless except for the cashier who is muttering to herself about crazy americanos as I wheel my shopping cart out with about twenty rolls of toilet paper and $200 worth of canned vegetables and fish. It is midnight when I fill two trash barrels with water in our shower.

'After the city services go down, we will be ready for the monsoon!' I tell Jackie as I tumble into bed. She is whispering something about craving a piña colada when my eyes close.

21 September, 11 am

The sky is low grey wool. The air tastes like hot broth and does not move. Neither does our landlord, and I am worried that his apartment building is going to come apart at the seams unless we start securing things. Radio WOSO says the storm is making a beeline for Puerto Rico. All preparations must be rushed to completion. The only good news is that Hurricane Georges has burned off a little energy; winds are down to 180 kilometres per hour, reports the weathered hippie who lives across the hall.

'What's that mean?' I ask.

'Maybe we won't lose the roof this time,' he chuckles. The hippie tells me he's on his fourth Medalla of the morning when he suddenly disappears from his balcony with a young woman in a filmy robe and a bottle of rum.

'There are grasshoppers in this world,' I think, 'and there are ants.'

I do not wait for the landlord to show up. I lower our awnings and close the shutters. Jackie takes Jake to our bedroom in the back of the apartment, a windowless concrete bunker whose design we have been at a loss to understand since we moved in. Now, I get the picture: it looks a lot like the *Last Days of Pompeii*.

21 September, 6 pm

The wind is at 140 kilometres per hour and climbing, according to the radio. Two seagulls fly backwards down the street. The water service gives up with a groan from the faucet. Minutes later, the electrical power dies with a wink of the lights and a growl from the air-conditioner. Out in the hall, the hippie and other hurricane veterans begin to gather. Someone knocks on the door. When I open it, a man hands me a beer and says, *'Viva la isla!'*

21 September, 8 pm

The gang out in the hallway has filled the stairs and landings from the second to fourth floors. They've got an arsenal of beer, pitchers of piña coladas and a CD player cranking out salsa to match the roar of the wind. Chico, who has evacuated the wooden penthouse on the roof above us, is telling the hippie, 'I heard a sound like a jet, man, and then the whole thing just sort of took off.' I think he is talking about his roof. Outside several awnings disintegrate with a sharp rip. For a second or two the music in the hall stops. Someone says, 'Carumba!' ... then the click of salsa begins again.

Back in our bunker, Jake snoozes in his crib while his parents, the americanos, eat cold tuna by candlelight. Inspired by my free beer and the sounds of the *salseros* partying in the stairwell, I make us a stiff piña colada and promise my beloved the stars if we ever get through this.

'Your timing's way off, Valentino,' she says.

21 September, 10 pm

The radio says the wind is blowing over 180 kilometres per hour at the airport when the instruments pack it in. Sixty houses are gone in Fajardo. Windows in the city's high-rises are popping like flashbulbs. Overhead something – probably Chico's penthouse – is crashing around on the roof like thunder. The whole building has begun to shake. I am hugging my family – swearing that our next assignment will be some place with a predictable climate, like England – when a loud bang sounds from the ceiling. Five more explosions follow in quick succession. There is a second of screeching metal, the pressure cracks in my ears, and I wait for the roof to go.

But there is only the whir of wind as the building stops trembling.

'What happened?' asks Jackie.

I am guessing that we just lost the rest of the penthouse or the TV antennas, when I hear a stampede of *salseros* in the hallway heading up the stairs to the roof. There is a knock on our door.

'Come on out, americanos. You can see the moon!'

Cautiously, we decamp from our bunker and follow the party up to the roof. The wind has already faded to a waltz. Amazingly, most of Chico's penthouse is still intact, and he is passing out beers to the gang. We stand on a naked roof, where once there was a forest of TV antennas, and look out over the ancient city, glowing like an El Greco painting of Toledo.

'*Existe!*' sighs a woman. Maybe she means THE CITY still exists or WE still exist. I can't tell . . . and it doesn't matter. At this point both seem miracles.

As Jake babbles a lullaby to the stars, his mother coils her arm around my waist and suggests we share that piña colada.

'*Viva la isla!*' I think.

22 September, 3 pm

According to the radio, the whole island is without electricity and will be for weeks. More than a third of all homes and businesses have been destroyed or damaged. Estimates put losses at $15 billion. Since Puerto Rico is a commonwealth of the United States, this disaster ranks as the most costly in US history – the Storm of the Century.

But only five people on this island of 3.8 million citizens have died in Hurricane Georges, and now it is a dry, sunny afternoon. Already there are traffic jams as islanders abandon the heat and destruction of their neighbourhoods to head for the beaches, a swim and the fresh trade winds. Jackie, Jake and I are among them. At Piñones, the breeze tickles the skin. María's shack is gone. But she is here selling cold Medalla from a cooler to a crowd of smiling survivors. As she passes out the beer, we can hear her chanting, '*Viva la isla!*'

'Readiness is all,' interprets Jackie.

We queue up for a beer . . . like there is no tomorrow.

Service all hours

Scott McNeely

Scott was born and raised in Los Angeles, California, and is actually fond of the place. After graduating from UC Berkeley, Scott spent a few years living in San Francisco, New York, Dublin and Istanbul. He eventually grew homesick for the Golden State and returned to San Francisco in 1997. Scott co-authored Lonely Planet's *Czech & Slovak Republics*, *USA* and *Europe on a shoestring* guides, and has written chapters on Romania and Ireland for other Lonely Planet books. He vaguely remembers careers as an editor and executive editor, but only vaguely.

INISHMÓR is one of three sparsely inhabited islands off the western coast of Ireland, the others being Inishmaan and Inisheer. Part of the Aran Island chain, it's a popular summer destination; in winter, however, it's a lonely scrap of limestone buffeted by violent Atlantic storms, its few narrow lanes lashed by rain, its harbours and beaches pounded by rough surf.

In summer the island's population swells by the thousands, thanks to a steady gush of tourists; come winter, Inishmór slows to a crawl. Only a few hundred stoic islanders manage to scrape a living year-round, tending to fields or manning the lines on worn fishing trawlers. At this time of year the number of tourists can often be counted on one hand.

On a cruel February day in 1990, Inishmór's hand had only three fingers – an elderly German couple and myself, the fresh-faced American studying in Dublin for a year. My ferry from Galway had pitched and rolled through howling wind and pounding rain into the relative sanctuary of Kilronan, Inishmór's ambitiously named 'capital': a village with three paved roads, four pubs and a fish and chippie.

Despite the bleak landscape, I was far from disappointed by Kilronan. Not after an hour-and-a-half crossing from Galway that had brought me to the brink of green-faced nausea. Earlier that morning the owner of my Galway B&B had cooked up a 'wee breakfast': two fried eggs, two sausages, two thick strips of bacon, three fried tomatoes, circles of black and white pudding, endless toast and tea, and the obligatory bowl of cornflakes. 'Go on and eat,' she'd commanded. 'You'll need it for the crossing.' I feigned fullness more than once, but it was obvious that a clean plate was the only conceivable outcome.

An hour later I was standing on the deck of a ferry feeling violently ill. The boat was still docked and yet my breakfast was on the verge of tumbling into the sea. More than once I considered jumping onto dry land and catching the next bus back to Dublin. As the crew made their final preparations I even grabbed my bag and took a few tentative steps toward the gangway, only to feel the ship heave up on a swell, slamming me to the deck.

I picked myself up and made a second attempt at the gangway. Only a few more steps and I'd be back on dry land. But fate intervened and I received an urgent message from my stomach. Retching repeatedly into the Atlantic, I watched Galway disappear behind a sheet of rain. I cursed the ferry, I cursed Irish cooking, and I cursed my rotten luck. In retrospect this was merely Act I in my Irish island nightmare.

A week before I had even heard of Inishmór, my one true love left a note for me in our flat. It kindly requested my presence later in the day at a Dublin pub. The note went on to say that we desperately needed to have a talk.

Now most men will instantly perceive the gravity of that phrase – 'have a talk'. Girlfriends don't generally schedule talks unless there is something very serious to talk about. In our case, I had a bad feeling that the subject of our talk would be relationships. More specifically, our relationship and why it was foundering.

It turned out to be worse than I thought. I was informed in no uncertain terms that 1) I was a lousy boyfriend, 2) I was a lousy lover, 3) I was hopelessly immature, and other things which I don't care to remember. The catalogue of my faults took up the better part of an afternoon, ending with a stunning announcement. Unbeknownst to me, my one true love had been seeing a mutual 'friend'. After a two-year relationship with me, she was in love with somebody else. After two years of misery, she was now happy and fulfilled.

As I sat digesting this bit of news, my one true love said goodbye with a noncommittal hug and a thin kiss on the lips.

Never one to sulk, I decided to take immediate and decisive action. I got rip-roaring drunk. The kind of drunk involving naughty bar-room singing and one-line jokes of questionable taste, not to mention reckless socialising with all the wrong people.

Through a thick haze of booze, I met a fellow who had a friend who knew somebody whose uncle owned an empty cottage on the island of Inishmór. According to my new best friend, the door needed no key and as long as I didn't mind drafts (something about a missing roof?) this friend's friend's uncle's cottage would be the perfect place to contemplate life, love and the unfairness of it all. I think he said that it was a small whitewashed home a few miles beyond Kilronan, two quick turns past a shrine to the Virgin Mary. Easy to find – just ask for the O'Connor house. Or maybe he said the O'Donnells. Or perhaps it was the Fitzpatricks.

My first hour on Inishmór was fairly disheartening. Nobody in the village had ever heard of my friend's friend's uncle, nor had they heard of a cottage with a door that needed no key. The barman told me further that although he wasn't familiar with secret doors and magical cottages, there was a B&B just down the lane.

In an instant I was back out in the rain, fighting uphill against the wind in search of the B&B, which turned out to be very pleasant. The kindly owner ushered me into her parlour and sat me in front of the fire. She poured cups of tea and produced a plate of biscuits. After a few sips I felt completely at home; so much so that I soon stumbled upstairs to my room to snuggle between the crisp white sheets of a most inviting bed.

I have often found that nothing can compare to a soft, warm bed on a vicious winter's day. Howling winds and drenching rains are nothing when you're tucked safely beneath a heavy blanket and a pile of hand-knitted quilts. As my head sank deep into the pillow, it seemed I had turned the proverbial corner after enduring one of the worst weeks of my life. I was on the road to rest, relaxation and recovery.

10 pm. Scratch. Toss. Turn and scratch.

10.15 pm. Scratch. Scratch again. Full toss, reverse toss, scratch.

10.18 pm. Long sweeping scratches along left thigh. Short, furious scratches up and down right leg, right calf, left thigh.

10.19 pm. Deep digging scratches across entire body. A last valiant effort at sleep.

10.20 pm. Eyes wide open. Massive full-body scratch and the creeping realisation . . .

In an instant I jumped from the bed and stood stark-raving naked in a pitch-black room, simultaneously scratching and fumbling for the light. I couldn't explain it, yet the sensation was undeniable. Every square inch of flesh was registering the pricks of a thousand pins. Feet, legs, thighs and – oh no, please not that! – were all pulsating, absolutely screaming for relief.

Why had my body turned into one immense malicious itch? Had I been poisoned? Was I suffering from history's most violent allergic reaction?

The answer was all too obvious. By the naked light of the bedside lamp the riddle was laid bare: a mass of throbbing red welts told me I was a victim of the dreaded *Sarcoptes scabiei*, tiny mites that prey on human flesh, burrowing deep into the skin with their razor-sharp mandibles.

But that wasn't the worst of it. I wasn't contending with one or two of these nasty little beasts, but with dozens and possibly hundreds. Before my very eyes, large swathes of flesh were being harvested by troops of *Sarcoptes scabiei*. A trail of welts ran up my arms and down my legs. Each welt pulsated with a reddish rage, itching with an intensity that even now is difficult to describe. Picture the worst itch you've ever had and multiply it by a factor of 100 – that's only one welt. I had dozens scattered across my body.

Of course I panicked, who wouldn't? It was late on a rain-soaked night and I was on a small island off the coast of Ireland. A small island with three paved roads, six pubs and a fish and chippie – but not a single pharmacy! Though scabies can be treated with over-the-counter lotions, the nearest pharmacy was in Galway. The next mainland ferry didn't leave for another twelve hours – an eternity in my condition.

What to do? I had read that scabies were highly contagious. My sheets, my towel, the chair downstairs – unwittingly, I had transformed everything I had touched in the last few hours into a possible agent of infection. I panicked and, unforgivably, made a hasty escape.

Judging by the greeting I received at the pub, I must have looked like an escaped convict. There was the very same barman I had met earlier that day, no doubt wondering what I was doing, bag in hand, at 10.30 pm on a stormy night. When I crossed to the counter and ordered a pint, he gave me a look brimming with suspicion.

The giveaway was my body language. Being careful not to touch anything or anybody, lest they become infected, I stood rigid at the bar while everybody else relaxed on bar stools. It was fairly obvious that something was amiss.

After my first pint I ordered a second, and a third. By the fourth, I was feeling sozzled, and the itch wasn't as intense. Which led to me think, maybe I was overreacting. Maybe I only had a minor case. Perhaps I wasn't infected at all. It could be nothing more than a bad case of fleas.

Whatever it was, I was feeling confident enough to anchor my elbows on the bar, contagion be damned. I laughed at a few jokes and made small talk with a man down the bar. This was a tactical error on my part, for when he finished his pint and pulled on his coat, he walked over and gave me a friendly pat on the back, a half-hug that took me fully by surprise. My face instantly turned pale and I blurted out, 'Don't touch me! Don't anybody touch me!'

In retrospect I can't blame those fine gentlemen in the pub for being offended by my sudden outburst. I don't begrudge them their anger. If I was mean-spirited I could take comfort in the knowledge that, as three or four of them pushed me out the door and into the night, a few tiny stowaways undoubtedly jumped ship and found fresh fleshy homes. But I am not mean-spirited, and I do feel remorse. Gentlemen of the pub, please accept my belated apologies.

As the sun began its upward creep the next morning, I woke to find myself shivering in a damp ditch. Ever the optimist, I pronounced the chilly dawn air to be a rare palliative. The itching was mostly under control. Dawn had arrived, the rain had stopped, and the ferry was due to leave in an hour. I was getting ever closer to Galway and its pharmacies.

Galway, oh Galway, third-largest city in Ireland and a thriving metropolis compared to the huddled villages of Inishmór. As the ferry pulled into Galway Bay, my body registered an intense jolt of relief. In a city of 50,000 people I was sure to find some relief, physical and mental. In my mind I was already at a pharmacy loading up on napalm-strength lotion, stepping into a warm shower, crawling into bed for an honest night's sleep.

Is life ever that simple? Of course not. Instead of jumping off the ferry and into the arms of the nearest pharmacist, I found myself contemplating a worst-case scenario: Sunday in the Republic of Ireland. A holy day in a country that takes its holy days seriously. On a Sunday there wasn't a chance in hell that a single shop would be open. I felt it in my bones. Perhaps a zealous café-owner would break free from Mass and fire up a greasy grill. A few publicans would no doubt pour pints for thirsty churchgoers. But a pharmacist plying their trade on the Day of Rest? Not a chance.

I made straight for the tourist office. Closed. Across Eyre Square to a newsagent. Closed. Down William Street to a coffee shop. Closed. All of Galway was buttoned up tight. I was getting desperate, desperate enough to contemplate jumping naked into

Galway Bay in order to freeze the critters into submission. I could build a fire and burn them off. If all else failed I would numb my senses by drinking copiously for twenty-four hours.

At the end of Shop Street I met an elderly woman on her way to Mass, but my request for directions to the closest pharmacy drew a blank. On Sunday, she protested, everything's shut for the day. Yes, yes I know. But surely there *must* be a 24-hour pharmacy in Galway. This is a major city in a modern European country. A 24-hour pharmacy absolutely must exist.

The friendly church-going woman agreed. Yes, there *ought* to be a 24-hour pharmacy in the great city of Galway. But no, such a thing does not exist. You could try the all-night chemist in Salthill, but you'll find nothing of the sort in Galway.

Salthill, sweet music to my ears. With indescribable relief I pounced on the poor lady and squeezed the details out of her. What was the name, what was the address, which side of the street was it on, what was the fastest route. Unfortunately, her memory wasn't all it should be. She was certain I would find an all-night pharmacy in Salthill. As to the street, she suggested I try Whitestrand Avenue. If it wasn't there I was to try Upper Salthill Road and then Lower Salthill Road. Middle Street? No, definitely not Middle Street.

With the blind faith that only comes with old age, she was certain I would find my pharmacy, if only I looked hard enough. So off I went, hurtling down High Street, crossing the River Corrib, sprinting down Sea Road. On that quiet Sunday morning, my pounding footsteps sounded like violent thunderstorms, crashing off doorways and echoing down empty alleys.

I finally came tumbling into Salthill delirious with expectation. I crashed down main roads and tore up lanes. Whitestrand Avenue was a blank. So too were Upper and Lower Salthill roads, not to mention lowly Middle Street.

And then I saw it – salvation disguised by an unremarkable storefront halfway down the street. An honest-to-goodness pharmacy. A beautiful medicinal warehouse with a sign in the window promising 'Service All Hours', daily from 10 am to midnight.

Running the gauntlet

John Mock

John first trekked in the Karakoram and Hindukush in 1977. Since then, he has spent most of his time in Pakistan, India and Nepal, studying, working and trekking. During that time John also earned a PhD in South and South-East Asian Studies from the University of California, Berkeley. He lives with his wife and Lonely Planet co-author, Kimberley O'Neil, in northern California.

PAKISTAN,' lamented the reporter for the Islamabad daily newspaper, 'is nowhere on the world tourism map.'

'It used to be,' I mused. 'Back when the overland route from Europe to India and Nepal went through Afghanistan and Pakistan. But there's fighting in Afghanistan and now everybody flies into Delhi or Kathmandu.'

'Who would come to Pakistan?' muttered the reporter. 'The law and order situation is frightening. It's futile, even grotesque, to ask tourists looking for fun to choose Pakistan as their next destination.'

'Grotesque,' I thought, 'may just be the right word for it.'

The wild side. It's what attracts Pakistan's few fun-seekers these days – mountain climbers, hard-core adventure trekkers and the steady trickle of overland travellers making their way between Kashgar and Islamabad along the Karakoram Highway, or KKH as it is commonly known. There's fun to be had up there in northern Pakistan's Karakoram and Hindukush mountains, but to get there you have to run the gauntlet of the KKH, where Mother Nature is against you. Basically, the mountains are trying to reclaim the road and wash it into the Indus River. The Indus winds its way from western Tibet though Central Asia, then cuts through the Karakorams and around the western end of the Himalaya, following the fault line where the Indian subcontinent and the Asian landmass collide. This fault line is one of the most seismically active zones on the planet.

The 'highway' itself, hardly more than a ribbon of broken tarmac, is seasonally assaulted by monsoon rains, mudslides and landslips. Section after section is reduced to corrugated gravel and bare earth by the constant slipping and sliding. There's no stopping gravity and natural erosion. In my travels, I've come to expect the occasional rain of rock on the vehicle roof and to encounter massive boulders blocking the road. At such places, I just get out of whatever vehicle I happen to be travelling in, grab my bag, pick my way over the rubble and climb into whatever vehicle is stopped on the other side. During particularly bad weather, I've had to change vehicles four or five times. Sometimes I've arrived at a recent landslide to find other travellers retrieving the lifeless bodies of those unfortunates who tried to cross and were caught in the hail of boulders.

The only alternative is the daily Islamabad–Gilgit flight on Pakistan International Airlines, or PIA. Not much of an alternative, since the planes operate maybe only one-third of the time. The airplanes themselves are old Fokker Friendship twin-engine propeller jobs, with a ceiling of 4500 metres. They have no chance to fly above the clouds and in bad weather can only wait in Islamabad for a better day. It can be as much as a week between flights, and there's not much else to do but wait, because even the KKH could be closed by weather-induced slides or rockfalls. Planes that have tried to make it by flying close to the ground just under the clouds have disappeared, probably swallowed without trace by the Indus River and ground into dust to be deposited into the Arabian Sea. I've come to hate those white-knuckle flights to Gilgit during breaks in the monsoon. The plane lurches violently through gaps in the clouds, just clearing a 4000-metre mountain pass with enough visibility to avoid running into the mountains on either side. You have to wonder whether the planes can keep taking such poundings. With the Fokker company now out of business, PIA keeps its fleet in the air by cannibalising the planes. So when the tyre on the nose wheel blows out because the pilot comes in a little too hard, well, maybe next time the strut will crack, and eventually, there won't be any of those old planes left to fly. Maybe then Pakistan will lengthen the Gilgit runway to accommodate small jets. The necessary land just sits there, vacant, a grazing ground for cows and goats at the end of the runway. But the Gilgit Valley is so narrow jets would barely clear the steep rock walls. So nothing happens, and the KKH is always there, the gauntlet waiting to be run, beckoning with its promise of a ride straight through.

So you get into the bus or minivan to make the trip. Don't forget to check the tyres first! And just who is the driver? When was the last time he had a night's sleep? To earn the extra rupee, drivers will make several trips back-to-back. As you ride along the road, you can see the result: the twisted wreckage of unlucky vehicles lies along the river below the KKH at sharp turns, where the drowsing driver woke too late to keep on the road and plunged in a moment of terror over the edge, sometimes into the Indus, sometimes onto the rocky bank. One bus went into the river with forty-five passengers on board, and they never found even so much as a seat cushion.

Yes, that's the KKH, and no matter how cautious you are, no matter how many questions you ask, there's always an element of chance. You just hope and pray that a boulder doesn't fall on you, that the big truck approaching gives you enough room to get by on the high narrow road, that you don't become an incidental victim of the mountains' continual effort to reclaim the road, a casualty of the natural process. In Pakistan, such events are regarded as God's will. Small stone slabs set along the roadside announce the danger zones with a masterfully understated word or two in blue paint, such as 'Good luck' at the start of a bad section, or a comforting 'Relax' at its end.

The KKH is the vital link between Islamabad, where international airlines arrive and depart and trekking permits are obtained, and Gilgit, the departure point for treks into the surrounding mountains. There's just no avoiding it and the hazards it brings. And as if the natural hazards weren't enough, there are human hazards as well. Natural hazards are to a certain degree predictable – if it rains, there'll be slides and rockfalls, and everyone knows it would be best not to get into one of those small night vans. But the human hazards are not so easy to predict. A local issue may flare up and bring hundreds of men onto the KKH in some small town, blocking traffic and threatening to close the road unless the government yields to their demands.

In 1994, while researching *Trekking in the Karakoram & Hindukush* for Lonely Planet, I found myself in Gilgit at the end of the season. I was preparing to head down to Islamabad for the winter, when I heard that Islamic militants had constructed ten barricades on the KKH between Chilas and Thakot, in the region known as Indus Kohistan. Shouting '*Shariat ya Shahadat*' (Islamic law or martyrdom), they were demanding immediate enforcement of Islamic law in their part of Pakistan. At Thakot, where the KKH bridges the Indus, over 8000 armed militants, many of them veterans of the Afghan war, had blocked the road. All traffic up and down the KKH was brought to a stop, and food supplies were beginning to run short in Gilgit. In the neighbouring valleys of Swat and Bajaur, news reports warned that the militants had seized the main airport in Saidu Sharif, and were holding local officials hostage. Even more alarming, the Pakistan army was planning a full-scale assault to dislodge the militants, who were against everything they termed 'anti-Islamic'. One news report carried a list of those things they found offensive. Along with the usual demands for the establishment of Islamic courts and the appointment of elder white-bearded judges, my eye stopped on a declaration that left-hand drive cars were anti-Islamic, and even wearing a watch on the left wrist was anti-Islamic! Were they serious? What if they checked travellers along the KKH and pulled aside all those wearing watches on their left wrist?

'This,' I thought, 'is one time I think it would be better to wait for the flight rather than try the road.'

After seven days, I heard that the army had used helicopter gunships to dislodge the militants in Swat, and several army columns had attacked those in Bajaur. The militants had responded with rocket and mortar fire from their hilltop positions. After a few days it was over, but I waited for the flight and hoped the militants didn't have any shoulder-launched Stinger anti-aircraft missiles to target a PIA plane.

Now when I drive up the KKH, a painted slogan on the wall of a house overlooking the road proclaims, 'Proud to be an Islamic fundamentalist'.

There's no doubt the KKH is vital to Pakistan. The government will not long tolerate any closure of the road, be it by natural or political forces. They have built a series of fort-like police stations all along the road. Built of thick grey stone, with a single tall turret, these muscular posts are designed to hold off any siege by irate locals. Most of the posts maintain a barrier which can be raised or lowered at will, stopping all passing vehicles to be registered. The police at the posts also record the nationality and passport number of any foreigners in the vehicles.

Shortly after the militant activity, I travelled through the KKH in a small van that had been hired by a disparate group of trekkers. We were all heading for Islamabad after several months in the mountains, feeling rather pleased with ourselves for organising a van that would take us directly to Islamabad in some sort of comfort.

As we passed through Shatial, one of the small roadside towns that the militants had occupied, a policeman motioned for us to stop. Our driver slowed, and rolled down his window. The KKH was barely wider than the vehicle, so we found ourselves halted right in the middle of town. Bearded tribesmen passed all around the van, some with rifles slung over their shoulders, as the policeman spoke to our driver. Years of living in Pakistan had given me fluency in Urdu, and I prided myself on my ability to hold my own in conversation. The policeman asked the driver to take him some fifty kilometres down the road to the district headquarters. I leaned across the driver and greeted the policeman, and said to him in Urdu, 'I'm sorry, sir, but our van is full, and we don't have any room for you to sit.'

The policeman looked at me, and his lips slowly curled into a sneer.

'No room for me? No room for me in your van? Well, if there's no room for me in your van, then there's no room for your van on MY road!'

As he spoke, his face grew livid, and he drew himself up to his full height. He unsnapped his holster and withdrew his revolver. Brandishing it in the air, he began to utter curses and threats, vowing that we would never travel on his road and that rude foreigners should be expelled from his country. The tribesmen turned to look,

147

and the policeman knew he was on centre stage as a crowd began to gather around our van. The driver quickly pulled the keys from the ignition before the policeman could grab them. I tried to apologise, but the driver turned to me and sighed, 'Enough. Don't say anything.'

Sheepishly I sat back in the van, vowing not to put my foot in my mouth ever again. It took about an hour to pacify the angry cop, and we ended up squeezing him in next to the driver. It was, after all, his road. The cop was just another force of nature, another all too real hazard along the KKH.

New Year's Eve in Borneo

Chris Rowthorn

Chris was born in England and grew up on the east coast of the United States. He moved to Japan in 1992 and immediately fell in love with the country. After doing the obligatory few years as an English teacher, he landed a job at the *Japan Times*, which eventually led to a job at Lonely Planet. He has worked on Lonely Planet's *Japan*, *Tokyo*, *Hiking in Japan*, *Read This First Asia*, *Malaysia*, *Singapore & Brunei* and *South-East Asia*. He has travelled widely in Asia and escapes whenever possible to Thailand or Nepal. When not travelling, he lives a quiet domestic life in Kyoto with his wife, Chiori, commuting to the public bath and eating at *yakitori* restaurants.

N December of 1996 I travelled with two friends, Anthony and Denise, to Sarawak's Gunung Mulu National Park, on the island of Borneo. After exploring the caves and peaks of the park, we joined an English couple to attempt the colourfully named Headhunter's Trail, a backdoor exit from the park that involves travelling overland through the jungle to a tributary of the Medalam River. Our guide for the trip was a young man of the indigenous Iban people called Mr Larry. After leading us for three days through the jungle, we were met at the river by Mr Larry's father, Mr Siga, who bundled us into a riverboat for the trip down to his longhouse where we planned to stay the night. As we made our way downriver, it dawned on us that it was 31 December, New Year's Eve.

The first sign of what was to come came in the form of a dull roar emanating from the longhouse, which was as yet invisible beyond the riverbank. As soon as we pulled alongshore, we were met by several men from the longhouse who appeared to be astonishingly drunk. We tried out a few of the Iban greetings that Mr Larry had taught us but they just stared at us, swaying back and forth and saying nothing. Ignoring their cool reception, we climbed the riverbank, packs in hand, and made our way across a field to the longhouse. It was an impressive building, built on stilts and stretching a good 150 metres from end to end. People were milling about, including a circle of men placing bets on a cockfight. In addition to the scheduled combatants, an army of regular chickens joined a motley assortment of dogs in patrolling the longhouse grounds.

Mr Larry and his father ushered us up the steps of the longhouse as gangs of curious children stood by to watch. We crossed the veranda, the common area of the longhouse, which resembled nothing so much as the world's longest bowling alley. A row of lookalike doors fronted onto the veranda, each of which led to a single family dwelling. Since Mr Larry was our guide, we would stay in his father's house. It turned out that Mr Siga was chief not only of this longhouse, but of two others nearby – making him one of the highest-ranking Iban in Borneo. The chief's house was very well appointed indeed, with a stereo, a TV, a few comfortable chairs and a display case filled with family pictures. It could have been the living room of a middle-class family just about anywhere in the world; unless of course you looked out the window and saw the teeming rainforest spreading in every direction.

As soon as we sat down, Mr Larry produced a plastic bottle containing a murky white fluid. 'This,' he said proudly, 'is *tuak*, the drink of the Iban people.' Cups were filled and, after a welcoming toast by the chief, we took our first sip. While I had imagined it would taste something like Kentucky moonshine, it was actually quite good, like a sweet sake without the paint-thinner aftertaste. As we drank, the bigwigs of the longhouse filtered in one by one, eager to meet the exotic visitors from abroad. Many of them spoke surprisingly good English, including one man who introduced himself as Alfred. Soon after sitting down, he embarked on a long and somewhat convoluted speech in praise of Bill Clinton. Being a Democrat, I told him that I agreed with everything he had to say. With that, Alfred turned to me and with a great smile on his face announced, 'You and me, we drink together!' And to seal our new friendship, he lifted one giant hamhock of a hand and smacked it down so hard on my leg that I toppled over and spilled my *tuak* all over the floor.

Soon we were ushered into the dining room. My new friend joined us, whether invited or not we couldn't tell. Mrs Siga served up a wonderful meal of river fish, rice, local vegetables and, of course, huge pitchers of *tuak*. As we ate, we were repeatedly urged to 'Take rice. Take rice.' I would later come to regret not having taken enough rice.

After dinner, as we sat around the table, we were asked to sing a song. We looked at each other in horror – did we know even one complete song between us? After a brief discussion, we settled on the inevitable and launched into dimly remembered Beatles classics such as 'Yesterday' and 'Yellow Submarine'. Our hosts took this as well as could be expected, given our wretched singing voices and poor grasp of the lyrics. (If I recall correctly, we simply repeated the refrain of each song over and over until they could stand it no longer and cried out 'New song please!') Regardless of our trouble with the lyrics, we couldn't help grinning madly at each other – here we were having a Beatles singalong with the Iban people in the middle of Borneo on New Year's Eve.

Meanwhile, the *tuak* kept flowing. Spurred on by my ingrained self-destructive instincts, I was lured into making extravagant claims to Alfred about my drinking prowess. This was like pouring gasoline onto a fire. While Anthony and Denise begged off for a post-dinner nap, Alfred dragged me to another house, which doubled as the longhouse bar. He barked something to the old man who ran the place and moments later a great jug of *tuak* appeared before us. This was some of the best in Borneo, Alfred informed me, although by that point the subtleties of *tuak* were largely lost on me. Even though we were literally hurling down glass after glass, Alfred explained that this was just a warm-up. After midnight the real party would begin, and we would traverse the whole length of the longhouse, stopping for a glass of *tuak* at every single door. 'How many doors are there?' I enquired grimly. 'Only forty-five!' Alfred announced with a big smile on his face.

Let me take a moment here to tell you about Alfred. He was big for an Iban – close to two metres tall and somewhere between portly and downright fat. I'd guess that he was about thirty-five, but he could have been ten years on either side of that figure. He wore a perpetual grin and I got the impression that he did whatever he pleased, whenever he pleased.

As we sat there drinking, I noticed that all the adults were leaving the longhouse. 'Where are they going?' I asked Alfred.

'Oh, they go to church,' he said.

Before long, it was clear that the only adults left in the longhouse were me, Alfred and the rheumy-eyed old man who kept bringing out the *tuak*. Perhaps out of guilt for skipping mass, Alfred then embarked on a long series of pious Christian platitudes. He did not, however, find it odd that while every other adult in the longhouse was off praying and singing hymns, he should be steadily downing *tuak*.

At around 10 pm, Anthony and Denise found their way down to where Alfred and I were drinking. They looked sober and refreshed. I, on the other hand, was extremely drunk. Before long, church let out and the adults came flooding back into the longhouse, eager to start the festivities. We left the longhouse bar to join the party on the veranda. Up and down its length, knots of people were gathered in furious *tuak*-drinking sessions. Being the only outsiders, we were in great demand at these gatherings and people were literally fighting each other for the honour of our presence. Alfred clearly enjoyed the prestige that came from being the chaperone of these exotic foreign visitors.

By 11 pm the party had reached fever pitch. People clustered round us, madly trying to engage us in conversation. One man wanted to talk about durians. Another wanted to introduce us to his dog. Still others simply wanted to offer us *tuak*, which they invariably referred to as 'the local wine'. Presiding over this mad talk-fest was Alfred, who was clearly in his element. He took to translating everything we said for the benefit of those who didn't speak English. However, he often lost track of who spoke what language and, carried away in a manic polyglot frenzy, addressed me in Iban, translated what he had said into English for the tribal elders and then translated that again into Bahasa Malaysian for the children who stood nearby. Sometimes he managed this feat several times in the course of one long sentence, and there were times when I could have sworn that he was speaking three languages all at the same time. Of course, being completely drunk, everything he said made perfect sense to me.

The flock of children gathered round stared at us with rapt expressions. One of the bolder little boys approached me and ventured a shy 'Hello.' When I asked him his name, he smiled and said, 'Diego Maradona.' I thought the kid was pulling my leg, but then Denise said, 'No, they've all got names like that. I just met a girl named Cinderella.' It turned out that almost all the kids in the place were named after foreign movie stars and sports players. It was, I must admit, a strange feeling to be drinking *tuak* in Borneo with Cinderella and Diego Maradona.

Caught up in the drinking and talking, I lost all track of time. Suddenly, the revellers struck up a rather alarming chant: 'Get the gun! Get the gun!' For a horrible moment, I was afraid that I had committed some terrible breach of etiquette and would be made to suffer. However, they merely wanted to fire off a few rounds to ring in the New Year. Before I knew it, Alfred had dragged me to the railing of the veranda and placed a particularly fearsome-looking shotgun in the hands of the drunkest man in South-East Asia. After a brief argument about whose watch told the correct time the countdown began, and as the hour struck midnight, I pulled the trigger. The gun kicked viciously against my shoulder, and I was momentarily deafened, but it was worth it to see the smiles on the faces that swam in and out of focus around me.

Now that we had had properly rung in the New Year, Alfred announced that it was time to start drinking in earnest. I could hardly believe my ears. What did the man think I had been doing up until that point? Renewed supplies of *tuak* were brought forth and two men appeared with a miniature electronic organ and a couple of drums. As soon as they started playing, all but the oldest Iban jumped up to dance. At about this time Mr Larry reappeared. Throughout our trip, he had displayed an inordinate curiosity about Western music and dance styles. In particular, he was fascinated by the latest dance craze from South America, the lambada. Now, of course, he wanted me to demonstrate the latest dance steps from New York. This was a tall order indeed. I reached deep into my memory and brushed off a few vintage high-school prom gyrations which everyone emulated with glee. I felt like an aerobics teacher as they mirrored every horrible suburban dance step I could muster. Even now, I am sure there are Iban in Borneo who still practise my unique dancing style.

Before long, I was a sweaty mess. I begged off dancing for a while and wandered down the veranda to join another group of people busily consuming *tuak*. I was soon besieged by offers of 'the local wine', and was growing increasingly drunk by the minute. No, 'drunk' is far too mild a word. I was wrecked; swimming in a sea of *tuak* that seemed to know no end. However, the Iban clearly believed that you could never be too drunk. One young man, who was literally purple in the face, fell to the floor near where I was sitting. The people around him seized this opportunity to prop him up, force his mouth open and pour more *tuak* down his throat. This was greeted by great hilarity on the part of all present. I made a silent vow not to pass out, but passing out was becoming a very real possibility. The whole longhouse was slowly spinning round me and I felt a horrible nausea coming on. I knew that if I didn't get out of there fast, I was going to make a nasty mess of the veranda floor. I made my way down the longhouse steps and followed a plankwalk that disappeared into a swamp next to the longhouse. Here, I busily set about vomiting up everything I had eaten and drunk in the last six hours.

Of course, I was not so drunk that I didn't fear that some horrible jungle creature would pounce on me as I retched and groaned. However, it turned out that a far more insidious creature was stalking me. I felt the vibrations first – something big was coming down the plankwalk toward me. I looked up and to my horror there he stood: Alfred. He had found me. The fact that I was being violently ill didn't seem to register with him. 'Come, we go drink *tuak*!' he bellowed. Luckily, Anthony appeared just a few moments later and somehow managed to drag him back to the longhouse. As they disappeared into the darkness, Alfred shouted over his shoulder, 'Chris, I am waiting for you. When you come back, we drink more *tuak*!'

I was not tempted to join Alfred. In a thick drunken haze, I made my way back to the longhouse, peered down the veranda to make sure that no-one was looking, then made a quick dash for the chief's house. I stumbled into the empty house and crawled onto a mattress. The whole longhouse seemed to spiral about me. For a moment, I feared that I was going to have to run outside and be sick again, but there was so much alcohol in my bloodstream that unconsciousness quickly took precedence over nausea.

Just as I teetered on the brink of oblivion, something large grabbed my arm and hauled me halfway off the mattress. I opened my eyes to see Alfred staring down at me expectantly. 'Come,' he said. 'Now, we go to forty-five doors!' Even in my wretched drunken state I had to laugh. Was this man serious? Here I was, on the verge of going out like Keith Moon or Jimi Hendrix, and he was suggesting a nightcap of forty-five glasses of *tuak*! Needless to say, I did not take him up on his offer. As I sank back into unconsciousness, I had a grim vision of the Iban carrying my prostrate form down the length of the longhouse, stopping at each door to pour a glass of *tuak* down my unprotesting throat.

The next morning at 7 am, the sound of loud music woke me from a tortured sleep. 'It can't be,' I thought, 'they're not still at it.' But they were. The Iban had partied straight through the night. As for me, I was suffering from an apocalyptic hangover. Even the slightest movement caused rays of pain to shoot through my head. A quick New Year's resolution was in order. I vowed to myself, 'I shall not, as long as I live, consume another drop of alcohol. It is the bane of my existence. It is the root of all evil. It is the ink with which the fool signs his soul over to the devil. GET THEE BEHIND ME SATAN!'

Unfortunately, Satan was right in front of me. When I opened the door of the chief's house, an Iban man rushed forward with a glass of *tuak* in his outstretched hand and said, 'The local wine!' I took the cup, and I drank it. In a lifetime of short-lived New Year's resolutions, this was the shortest.

The local cure

Andrew Draffen

Andrew lives in Melbourne, Australia, with his Brazilian wife, Stella, and their two children, Gabriela and Christopher, whose great-great-grandfather introduced football to Brazil. Andrew is co-author of Lonely Planet's guide to Brazil, and he also contributed to the LP guide to South America. He spends an excessive amount of time daydreaming about sunsets on Ipanema beach.

RAIN in Rio causes confusion, especially in the minds of the city's inhabitants. Cariocas don't like it at all when it rains. They can't go to the beach, carouse in outdoor cafés or walk through the streets. There's simply nothing good to do.

Rain also causes traffic chaos, so catching the local bus to the central bus station from Ipanema through a flooded city rush hour meant I'd be cutting it fine. There was just enough time to grab a newspaper and bottle of water.

The bus ride to southern Bahia would take about twenty-four hours. As we left Rio, the sun was setting behind the Serra dos Órgãos range to the west, its jagged granite peaks silhouetted in the crimson sky.

The other passengers were mostly Bahians travelling home; they had already started laughing and joking, swapping stories and making friends for the long ride. I was exhausted from the weeks I'd spent researching, so the prospect of a long bus ride was strangely appealing. It would give me a chance to recharge after Rio.

In Brazilian buses there's often a driver's name tag in a slot above his head. Our driver's name was Paixão (passion) and he drove accordingly, eyes intent on the road, watching for every opportunity to overtake a slower-moving vehicle in front.

The newspaper headlines made it hard for me to relax. The day before, a fuel tanker had overturned on a busy highway in São Paulo, with two buses travelling close behind. The first had crashed into the flaming tanker. The second had managed to stop sixty metres from the fire, but had soon become enveloped in flame as well.

Almost all the passengers had been asleep. Some from the first bus had managed to escape through the windows – they had only thirty seconds. The passengers in the second bus had two minutes before the tanker exploded. One hundred and eight people were caught in the fireball: fifty-three died from burns or asphyxiation. It was one of the most tragic road accidents in Brazil.

The report went on to describe how some survived and others didn't. One little girl with a remarkable memory helped identify the bodies because she could remember exactly what everyone had been wearing. One of the victims, a young girl, had been wearing a T-shirt printed with the phrase *'Nada e coincidência, tudo e providencia'* (Nothing is coincidence, all is destiny).

I'd read enough. I looked up at Paixão. Would we make it OK? *'Se Deus quiser'* – as the Brazilians say – 'If God wishes'. I looked around, deciding which window to kick out in case of an emergency, before dozing off.

By dawn we were in the small state of Espírito Santo. I read a feature story describing how approximately 99% of the state's Atlantic rainforest had already disappeared, replaced by pastures and eucalyptus plantations. In Brazil these plantations are sometimes called 'green deserts' because they're devoid of animals and other plants.

I tried to read on, but slipped into the meditative, zombie state well known to veterans of long bus trips, staring out the window watching the scenery speed by. It wasn't much to look at – just pastures and eucalyptus plantations.

As we crossed into southern Bahia, a wave of nostalgia swept over me. It had been fifteen years since I'd travelled here. During that first trip I'd met my wife, Stella, in the small village of Trancoso. She'd been on vacation from her teaching job in the megalopolis of São Paulo, and her big blue eyes had knocked me out. I couldn't speak Portuguese and she spoke little English, but eye contact was enough. Little did we then know that fifteen years later we'd be living in Melbourne, Australia, with two kids and a mortgage!

But before I could retrace my steps to Trancoso there was Porto Seguro and Arraial d'Ajuda to visit. I couldn't believe Porto Seguro. The site of the first Portuguese landing in 1502, it now catered for huge numbers of Brazilian package tourists, who came to sit in beach bars all day, get plastered and go out at night to huge dance raves that lasted until dawn. When did they sleep? Who knows? I only had to find out where.

Leaving Porto Seguro, I crossed the river on the car ferry (fifteen years ago it had been by fishing boat) and caught a kombi to Arraial d'Ajuda. Compared to Porto Seguro, it was still a small town, but there were paved roads now, and a water park with slides and chlorinated swimming pools. All the locals were getting ready for the tourist season, when hordes of Paulistas, Cariocas and Mineiros would descend to watch sunsets and moon rises, dance at full-moon raves on the beach, smoke ganja and screw their brains out. Fifteen years ago it was already a party town. Other travellers had told me that if you couldn't get laid here you should take a gun and shoot yourself.

This time I wasn't trying to get laid, just get out as fast as I could. Trancoso was only thirteen kilometres if you walked via the beach, so the next day I left after breakfast. The first people I met along the beach were a naked Carioca couple who offered me a joint. The walk took me all day.

Trancoso brought back so many good memories. The *quadrado* (main square) looked as good as it ever did – a long grassy area with shady trees surrounded by rustic, brightly painted, single-storey buildings. At the far end, a simple white colonial church overlooked the sea from a high bluff. This was definitely the place to slow the pace.

It was early October and things were pretty quiet. Money was tight and the locals had stretched their credit to the limit. Everyone was waiting for summer. I was still adjusting to the slower rhythm of the Brazilian north-east, a pace which could make research difficult. Instead of answering questions directly, people would offer me a *cafezinho* and invite me to sit down and have a chat. This was frustrating while my head was still full of timetables and deadlines, but I eventually gave up and decided to relax for a couple of days, to slip into the slower (and infinitely more pleasant) rhythm of the north-eastern Brazilian coast.

The plan must have worked well on my brain, because it was three days before I noticed the thin red line on the sole of my right foot. At first I thought it may have been a *bicho do pé*, a nasty little parasite that lives in warm sand and burrows just under your skin. If you don't cut it out it starts to grow – and then you've got real problems. But I'd had a *bicho do pé* before, and this red line didn't fit the description.

I sought out a sage old fellow I had met in the last few days. He ran a bar on the *quadrado*, and was named Ulysses. Being named after an ancient Greek hero isn't out of place here. It's not unusual in the north-east of Brazil for people to name their children after anything that takes their fancy. One guy I met had called his son Chuva (Rain). Combinations of sun (*sol*) and sea (*mar*) – Marisol and Solimar – are popular for girls. The ex-mayor of Trancoso had three sons named Wellington, Washington and Wallace.

Ulysses, a lean, fortyish chap with a mop of black hair and a large moustache, was an excellent storyteller, and very knowledgeable about Brazil. He also mixed great *caipirinhas*. Born on a ranch way out west in Matto Grosso, Ulysses, like his Greek namesake, had travelled widely before settling with his family in Trancoso.

As soon as he saw the red line on my foot he grabbed it to take a closer look. '*Bicho geografico,*' he said, '*sem duvida*' (without a doubt). He told me it was a parasite that burrows under the skin, penetrating too far to be cut out. As it moves around it leaves a red trail that makes your foot look like a road map. It had to be removed or . . . ? When I asked him the consequences of ignoring the critter, he shook his head at the unthinkable.

I had flashes of it eating its way merrily through my bloodstream and vital organs. I thought about the famous Brazilian *candiru*, the only known vertebrate parasite in the world. This small, slender fish lives on blood – any kind of blood. It usually enters the gills of the host fish and feeds on its blood, but has been known to enter the urogenital openings of human bathers, guided by the flow of urine if they happened to have peed in the water.

After forcing its way into the chosen crevice, it locks itself in place using the spines on its gill covers. Understandably, this causes excruciating pain and massive bleeding, often leading to infection. And you still have to figure out how to get rid of it. Surgery is often the only solution, and that's not a pretty thought.

According to Ulysses, I had two options. I could travel back to Porto Seguro and buy some expensive cream from the *farmacia* or take the local cure. Ulysses grinned as he mentioned the local cure. It meant tying a block of ice to the sole of my foot and waiting a few hours for it to melt. By this time, the bicho would be frozen stiff – *estupidamente gelada* (stupidly cold).

Maybe it was the several *caipirinhas* I had already consumed, but I opted for the local cure. Images of 'the cure' becoming like a party, with people coming into the bar, chipping off bits of ice to put in their drinks, playing some music, laughing, dancing and generally having a good Brazilian time, whirled through my head.

Ulysses was very supportive, even organising for the ice to be picked up in Porto Seguro the following morning. By that afternoon I would be rid of the beast.

When the ice arrived it was just past 3 pm and I was ready. The red line on my foot had changed course and was heading toward my big toe. Ulysses tied my foot to the block of ice with a towel and a length of rope. I sat back to wait.

Within twenty minutes, my foot was excruciatingly cold and the temptation to stop was intense. Ulysses plied me with more *caipirinhas* and distracted me by telling stories about his only visit to São Paulo, several years before.

By this time, my foot was frozen numb, but the *caipirinha* anaesthetic was excellent. I was feeling no pain, and the ice had shrunk to the size of an orange. Ulysses pulled off the bandages and carefully examined the sole of my wrinkly white right foot. '*Matou – com certeza.*' Killed it for sure.

It was near dark and my foot glowed as the last golden rays of sun filtered into the bar. I couldn't see any red lines either, but there must have been some in my eyes because when I stood up, I keeled over and hit the floor.

I'd not only learned to slow down, but when to stop as well.

Run, don't hesitate!

Susan Forsyth

Susan is Melbourne-born and bred but has lived out of Australia for more than ten years. She tries to combine her Lonely Planet research and writing with motherhood. For the past four years, she has lived in the dramatic countryside outside a whitewashed village in Spain's southern region of Andalucía, which she finds has enough in common with Oz to keep homesickness at bay. Susan has co-authored LP books on Spain, Andalucía, Australia, Indonesia and Mexico with her husband, LP author John Noble. She also travelled extensively in the former Soviet Union, assisting John with his research.

WILL I, or won't I?'
I sat at my desk in the geography department of an Australian school, gazing at a map of Sri Lanka. The end of the school year was approaching and I was pondering whether or not to throw in my current job, and lifestyle, in exchange for volunteer teaching in Sri Lanka. The deal included living with a Sri Lankan family for a year, and virtually no salary. I had been accepted for the position. It was up to me.

My decision was eventually reached with the help of my boss in the geography department, who quipped: 'Go on, go. Live out our dreams. You've got no mortgage or commitments.' I gazed on dreamily at the map of the tear-drop shaped island, pretty drawings exaggerating the island's attractions. I traced my finger along the coastline and dreamt of palm trees, of bougainvillea, hibiscus and frangipani, of white sand and warm tropical waters, of Buddhist monks in their orange and brown robes, of terraced rice padi fields, of elephants . . .

I took my colleague's advice and a few months later headed off to Sri Lanka. What a year it turned out to be! I made lifetime friends – Australian, American, British and, of course, Sri Lankan. I experienced the beauty of this tropical island: its marvellous beaches and hinterlands dripping with exotic foliage; its high mountains where tea is grown and the Raj somehow lives on; its ancient cities and ruins; its high plains where you might spot a leopard. Being based with a local family, I also had a window through which to closely view Sri Lankan culture. Working with quiet, motivated, sari-clad students made a lovely change from teaching cheeky Australian adolescents. And, except for Saturdays, we only taught in the afternoons.

But over it all hung the cloud, and often danger, of the island's political/religious conflict between its Sinhalese majority and Tamil minority. Tensions erupted several times that year, much to the consternation of my family at home, though for the most part we volunteers weren't overly worried. Even now, several years later, the conflict drags on, peaking and troughing with considerable loss of life at times, but never nearing resolution.

I didn't encounter a gun-toting terrorist in Sri Lanka – though some of my friends did – but I did have an equally frightening experience, a near-death encounter with a rampaging elephant in the wilds of Sri Lanka's Yala East National Park. Elephants are highly visible in Sri Lanka. You see them adorned and bejewelled in religious festivals, but more often you see them working (hips swaying rhythmically as they carry large logs with their trunks or heavy loads on their backs), playing and bathing in rivers (overseen by their mahouts), in elephant orphanages where abandoned or orphaned elephants are taken in and cared for – and in the wild!

But before heading out to the untamed regions where wild elephants roam, I became acquainted with the inland town where I was to live and work. My dreams of living on the coast had been shattered by my appointment to Matale, a hot, mosquito-ridden small town with few sights, where little seemed to happen. The sole white person in town, I suffered severe culture shock for several months. At first, the locals were disappointed by my appearance – athletic, with a short, spiky hairdo, quite unlike the Princess Diana look-alike they'd expected. But they got used to me, and my comings and goings with my backpack.

Ultimately Matale's chief attraction was its proximity to other destinations, especially the sacred old capital and cultural centre of Kandy, where I headed whenever I had a few days off. I felt more relaxed in Kandy, with its quaint architecture, bustling market and almost perfect climate. I had more varied company and could sometimes even party a little.

At the end of my first term in Sri Lanka I headed off to Arugam Bay, Sri Lanka's fabled surf beach on the south-east coast. I travelled with a fellow teacher, also called Susan, and Eddie, a colleague based in Monaragala who constantly raved about Arugam Bay.

Susan and I made the journey in two parts, staying overnight in Monaragala at the end of a gruelling day's travel down from

Kandy, rounding countless hair-pin ends. I can still recall us screaming, strap-hanging on an unroadworthy bus as it screeched around the bends. Bus travel has always been hair-raising in Sri Lanka. So many close shaves!

Although the bus journey from Monaragala to Arugam Bay was on the flat, it was not without entertainment. The bus broke down and we were conscripted, along with the men, to push it whilst the sari-clad Sri Lankan women sat modestly inside.

Somehow, the bus got going, and after passing through several military checkpoints we finally reached Arugam Bay. It was as pretty and laid-back as we'd been led to believe. We stayed for a couple of weeks, in basic accommodation run by friends of Eddie's. To break the routine of swimming, diving under waves, reading, lying in the sun, walking, playing board games and generally hanging out, we planned an excursion to Yala East National Park which was much more remote and less visited than its larger well-known neighbour Yala West National Park.

We set off on our expedition to Yala East by bicycle at around 8 am. Our preparations, including hiring the bicycles and getting some food together, had taken since 5.30 am so I was exhausted before we even left, though the morning was still relatively cool. We were a group of four, two Susans, Eddie and a fellow volunteer called Mark; I was the eldest by several years. We cycled twenty-five kilometres south along the paved road to the village of Panama, passing rice padi fields and open country. From Panama, we made for Okanda, a dilapidated Hindu temple.

I was thankful to reach our destination, for the going was tough and the sun was hot. We were greeted by the temple priest, a short, balding man with bad teeth, dressed only in a mini-sarong. He made us tea, which went down a treat. After resting, we walked to the nearby beach, an isolated, wild, windswept stretch, reminiscent of Australia's magnificent coast. We swam, happy to immerse our aching bodies in the warm, salty surf.

When the sun's rays weakened, Mark suggested that it was a good time to head into the national park, the entrance to which was close by. We followed various paths, skirting enormous puddles, eventually coming to the edge of a lagoon. To my horror, there in front of me at the water's edge was a crocodile basking in the sun. I had never seen one in the wild. My heart thumped. Mark was curious to look at the reptile more closely, but I convinced him to forget it. We quickly retraced our steps.

We discovered the correct track to the park's entrance, only to find that the offices were unattended, the windows of the buildings smashed. This was obviously going to be a different experience from the organised jeep tours of Yala West National Park. As if from nowhere, a couple of local men appeared, and asked us if we wanted to see some elephants.

We walked into the park and immediately spotted an elephant feeding from some trees 200 metres in the distance. Mark took a photograph but was eager to take more, closer to the elephant. We quietly walked further along the path into the park. Mark took another photo. The Sri Lankans followed us. We continued walking, each step taking us closer to the elephant, but we were still at a safe distance, or so we thought. Another photo and, this time, the Sri Lankans warned us not to get any closer to the elephant. Mark ignored their warning, but I held back with Eddie and Susan. Maybe the elephant heard us whispering to one another – its trunk would have sensed us anyway.

Suddenly everyone but me started running. Apparently Mark had called out, 'Run, don't hesitate!' Fairly formal words in a crisis, but I didn't hear them. I did run, however, when I heard the thundering sounds of the elephant's feet closing in on me as it charged. I can't recall when I first heard the elephant's ear-splitting trumpeting.

The other five escaped its path but for some reason I turned to look this massive creature full in the face. I was momentarily mesmerised, till terror got me moving. I didn't want to die this way. Newspaper headlines flashed through my mind. 'Volunteer teacher trampled to death in Sri Lanka!' No, thank you! I dived to the left across the elephant's trunk, losing my left sandal in the process, as the elephant veered off to the right, crashing its way through the bushes.

Trembling, heart palpitating, and with only one shoe, I hopped along to join the other five who had congregated behind a clump of bushes. One of the Sri Lankans had blood pouring from his face, the result of colliding with the bushes in his efforts to escape the mighty animal's onslaught.

It seemed that we had disturbed a mother and her young calf. Stunned, and not at all sure that the incident was over, we waited behind the clump of bushes – no obstacle at all to a charging elephant, but our hiding place gave us comfort. We could hear the elephant trumpeting in the distance for some while. Eventually, we gingerly emerged from behind the bushes and crept along the path to make our escape, too scared to search for my missing sandal. We made our way back to the temple, foolish to have entered the park on foot in the first place.

I spent a restless night, terrified we'd encounter the elephant the next day beyond the park's boundary. The others kept teasing me, 'Elephants never forget.' And for those thirty kilometres we bicycled back to Arugam Bay, I believed them.

Fear and loathing in Tuva

Anthony Haywood

Anthony was born in Fremantle, Australia, in 1959. He first pulled anchor at eighteen to spend two years travelling through Europe and the USA. He studied literature and Russian language at university, and has worked in a number of positions as a technical writer, trainer and translator. Anthony moved to Germany in 1992, where he lives with his wife, Sylvia, and works as an author for Lonely Planet and as a journalist and translator.

WHEN it comes to Russian cities, Kyzyl is no gem even by Siberian standards. Hot, dry, swirling with dust and flat as a pancake, it is the capital of Tuva, an obscure republic in southern Siberia inhabited by a people who speak a Turkic language, have strong cultural links with Mongolia and are by and large Buddhists.

With a population of just over 300,000, Tuva is a poor region, and one that has often been at the mercy of its neighbours. It has variously been under Turkic, Mongolian, Chinese and Russian control, and has suffered the fate of being annexed by Russia twice within thirty years – the first time in 1914, when it was wrested from China and made a protectorate; the second in 1944, when Stalin turned it into the so-called Tuvinian Autonomous Region. In 1921, between annexations, it experienced a brief period of independence and was known as Tannu Tuva. The first Russians arrived in the 19th century and promptly began to dig up the Tuvan's gold, till Tuvan soil and sell the pelt of any Tuvan animal that happened to wander across a gun sight.

Interestingly, Tuva is one of the few regions in Siberia where you're more likely to hear the local language rather than Russian. Tuva is also famous for throat singing, or *khoomey*, a haunting method of singing in 'two voices' simultaneously, the one a low drone and the other high pitched and flute-like. Other Tuvan predilections are for cross-country horse races and wrestling. And if that isn't enough, Tuva is believed to lie in the geographical centre of Asia, and has an obelisk on the bank of the Bolshoy Yenisey River in Kyzyl to prove it.

I felt ambivalent towards this ugly capital. Still fresh in my mind was a tortuous, seemingly endless 415-kilometre journey across the Western Sayan Mountains in a clapped-out bus on the M54 between Abakan in Khakassia and Kyzyl. It had been a ten-hour trip punctuated by stops at every river crossing, where the driver had quenched his thirst with water and poured alarming quantities of brake fluid into the struggling bus.

After the beauty of the Western Sayan Mountains, Kyzyl was Armageddon. I checked into the Hotel Kyzyl, a decaying Soviet-era architectural time bomb with staff at reception who made foreigners fill out a hotel registration form in triplicate in Russian.

'Will you register my visa with the police?' I asked.

'Of course,' came the reply.

I made my way to my room and unpacked some food I'd bought in Abakan – cheese, bread, a couple of apples – but just as I was about to begin my meal, there was a knock at the door. Opening it cautiously, I saw a thin woman in her mid-twenties with closely cropped dark hair. Almost whispering, she apologised for the disturbance and said she would like to discuss something very important. If I had time, she prodded nervously. She introduced herself as my floor lady.

Curious, I invited her inside, sat her down on a pre-Revolutionary lounge chair that showed its innards, and asked her what the trouble was.

'You're a foreigner,' she began uneasily. 'You've lived outside Russia. I want to find out about working abroad.'

'Anywhere in particular?'

'Greece,' she decided. 'I want to work in Greece.'

At first I was surprised by her response. Why Greece? I asked myself. Did it have something to do with Alexander the Great's push into Asia Minor (we were too far north), or was it influenced by the calendar hanging in the manager's office? But then I remembered where I was. Siberia. And Siberia was exile. It was bitterly cold winters and short, often hot, summers. It stood for Decembrist deportees; Dostoevsky in chains, religiously flogged to a near-death experience (good for world literature, but lousy for the nerves); it was gold, oil, animal pelts, salt mines, fish-canning factories and small-time, corrupt building industries; it was permafrost and recalcitrant public authorities; Mafia hearses angle-parked on the pavement outside the best restaurants in town; radioactive contamination. It was great rivers plied by heavily riveted speed boats that had done service for thirty years. It was the place for everything that had been discarded. Sometimes, when I looked at the rubble, rusting iron and other scraps of civilisation, I had the feeling that Siberia had been turned into one enormous rubbish dump beyond the Urals. But it was one full of surprises.

'Greece is a member of the European Union,' I explained. 'What about the work documents?'

'Oh, that's no problem,' she insisted. 'I can get a passport; I just want to know what it's like.'

I gave my a floor lady an apple and a piece of bread loaded with soapy cheese. I said that unless she spoke Greek she was only ever going to find jobs as a cleaning woman. 'Wages are low in Greece, and a lot of women in your situation get caught up in some nasty stuff . . .'

'Oh, don't worry about that,' she said.

'Have you thought about France?' I asked. 'The weather's not bad, and the wages are a lot higher.'

She shrugged her shoulders and looked about the room, studied her half-eaten bread and cheese as if about to speak, but then merely shrugged her shoulders again. Then, just as unexpectedly as she'd arrived, she stood up, downed the rest of her bread, and headed for the door. 'Thanks for your advice,' she said without great conviction, apologised again for the intrusion, and vanished.

I never saw her again, and when later, bored, I went looking for her to say she should go to Greece if she wanted to, I found a different woman in the floor lady's office. This one was plump and middle-aged; she looked like the floor lady in a hundred hotels across Russia. When I asked her about her colleague, she had no idea who I was talking about.

I liked Tuva, but I didn't like Kyzyl. The rest of the republic was everything the capital wasn't: rural, sparsely populated, friendly. I spent some time travelling around the countryside, but then, as if drawn back by an invisible thread, I found myself putting up in the grey capital, again at the Hotel Kyzyl. I filled out another guest registration form in triplicate, and again asked the woman at reception whether she would register my visa for me.

'*Konechno* – of course,' she said, vigorously thumping my three forms with a rubber stamp. She placed me in the same room I'd stayed in a week earlier. I flicked on the light switch in the bathroom and greeted the cockroaches heartily like old friends.

That afternoon I visited some of the sights – the Centre of Asia Monument overlooking the Bolshoy Yenisey River, the local market and the Regional Studies Museum, which had a large if rather motley collection of stuffed animals and a map on the wall depicting where I might find them. There was also a model of the Arzhan burial mound, one of the republic's most important archaeological finds. The mound's layout said a lot about the way things used to be done in Tuva: the chief and his spouse were buried in the middle of the mound. Buried around them were their servants, and around the servants were buried 160 horses. I was pretty sure not all the participants had been volunteers.

By early evening I was giving serious thought to returning to Abakan and a comfortable bed in the Hotel Intourist. A private taxi seemed the best way to go. I wandered down the main street to a vacant lot where drivers offered rides, and was soon approached by a Russian who seemed to control a fleet of imported Japanese station wagons. I didn't want to commit myself until I'd seen the driver, and I was told that he would pick me up from my hotel at noon the next day.

The following day, at exactly midday, another knock sounded on my door. 'Abakan!' came a muffled cry. My would-be driver was a dark-haired, mustachioed Russian with suspiciously glazed eyes. Judging by the stench of alcohol, he'd reached critical mass. I politely declined, saying I had urgent business, and made my way back to the 'taxi rank'.

'Abakan,' I said to a friendly looking rotund Tuvan leaning against a picket fence away from the mob. 'Abakan?' he asked back, surprised. He jumped up and asked double the going rate for the trip with a full load of passengers. I haggled the price down, but I would have to wait on other passengers.

'How many?' I asked.

'One more passenger,' he assured me, taking my luggage hostage in the boot of an old Lada.

He took up post again on the footpath, resting against the picket fence, dripping Buddhist serenity.

We waited. We waited an hour. We waited for what seemed like an eternity. Suddenly, spotting an old woman dragging a striped plastic bag across the lot, my driver jumped up, set off hastily towards her, stumbled, almost fell, corrected the fall, lurched and, grasping his knee, set off again in an agonised limp across the road. After a few steps, he abandoned the idea and dragged himself back to his picket fence to assess the damage. It looked serious. My heart sank.

We waited. It was getting on for 3 pm, and I knew we'd need a good five hours in his Lada to reach Abakan. Noticing my restlessness, he hobbled over to reopen negotiations. This time he asked a ridiculously inflated price and said he'd do the run alone with me. I agreed to double my price if we left straight away.

'Now!' he assured me, and sat down unconvincingly in front of the fence. After speaking to a friend for a few minutes, he rose unsteadily to his feet and motioned me to follow him to the car.

Coaxing the engine to life, he pulled out onto the road, turned, and headed off in the wrong direction.

'Where are we going?' I asked. And, just to clarify matters, I repeated, 'Now?'

'Now,' he replied, 'but first we've got to pick someone up.'

I'd coughed up good roubles for a solo ride, only to learn that I would have company. We drove a couple of kilometres out of town and along a dusty road that ran first through scrub and then between rows of dilapidated wooden houses.

'Not far,' he tried to reassure me.

We reached a high iron fence and pulled into the driveway. Above us, standing on what must have been a high platform, a large cur, part German shepherd, slobbered and drooled in a mad barking frenzy. A blonde woman opened the gate and told us to wait a moment. We waited. Then some minutes later a small, dark-haired woman emerged with a young child that seemed to be either her son or grandson.

Her name was Irina, and her grandson, as it turned out, was called Ruslin. I realised I was in the Gypsy quarter of Kyzyl. Irina stowed a few belongings next to mine in the boot and the rest between us on the back seat. 'Be good!' she admonished Ruslin before he'd done anything, and nursed him on her lap.

Things got better. This time we set off in the right direction. We left town, crossed the Bolshoy Yenisey River and climbed the low foothills of the Western Sayan Mountains making small talk. Irina was going to Shushenskoe, a town of 20,000 or so inhabitants just to the south of Abakan. Her mother lived there. So had Lenin. He'd spent the years from 1897 to 1900 in exile there with his wife. Unlike us, he'd travelled there by boat from Krasnoyarsk – in a second-class four-berth cabin – and paid eight roubles ten kopeck for the experience.

I put Irina's age at around sixty. She had long jet-black hair, fine ivory-carved features and a graceful, composed air. More composed, in fact, than her teeth, for when she spoke I noticed that most of her front teeth were either missing or rotten beyond repair.

'I have to fill up,' my driver said after a while, pulling in at a petrol station. It had an abandoned look about it; a few pumps stood rusting in the forecourt as if they hadn't seen a drop since the Brezhnev era.

'*Benzin nyetu*,' my driver said, reading from a cardboard sign that hung on the building. No petrol. We tried our luck at a second and then at a third before pulling over to ask a hapless Russian whose car had broken down whether there was petrol further along the road.

'*Nyet*,' came the reply. I looked at the petrol gauge and my heart sank. It showed empty. A warning light glowed menacingly.

The driver decided to try his luck anyway, and drove on, steering us across low saddles of the mountains. We stopped at another station. *Benzin nyetu*. I was becoming irritated.

Irina laughed and took it all in her stride. Ruslin climbed over the seat towards me enthusiastically, only to be wrenched back with the admonition, 'Ruslin! Stop that!'

The driver shook his head in consternation. 'There's a GAI station up the road. Maybe we can get some petrol there.'

GAI is the abbreviation for *Gosudarstvennaya avtomobilnaya inspektsia*. It is the body responsible for policing the Russian roads. Considering the state of our vehicle, stopping there didn't sound like a good idea to me. But there was another reason why I wasn't keen on the idea. First and foremost was that GAI officers had a reputation for trying to squeeze money out of anything that moved.

The GAI station, like most of its brethren, was a hideous concrete dog box deposited at the roadside, seemingly in the middle of nowhere. But the emptiness deceived; we were in fact on the Tuvan side of the border with Khakassia. The GAI office seemed to double as a border post.

We made a bad first impression. Having pulled up near the dog box, my Tuvan driver, momentarily forgetting his knee injury, opened the door, set one foot on the ground, collapsed and, groaning miserably, rolled across the ground in full view of two GAI officers, who looked up through a window just in time to catch the final throws of this spectacular acrobatic display. They emerged cautiously, Kalashnikovs slung over their backs, and walked across the yard to where my driver lay making unnatural gurgling sounds.

'We've run out of petrol,' my driver said between gurgles, as if this might somehow explain his Tuvan triple somersault roll with knee clench. 'Can you sell us some?'

They shook their heads, ran their eyes across Irina, Ruslin and myself on the back seat, eye-balled the driver again sceptically, and said we'd have to look for a station up the road.

We decided to wait it out. 'Someone will give us petrol,' my driver assured me, as he limped over to a bench to make himself comfortable. 'A *Tuvan* will give us petrol,' he added with boundless faith.

'Why didn't he fill up in Kyzyl?' I asked Irina.

She shrugged her shoulders indifferently. 'Ruslin! Stop that!'

'I'll tell you,' I continued, growing increasingly agitated, 'because he's a fool.'

'*Benzin nyetu*,' she murmured.

183

'Not in Kyzyl,' I said.

'No. All the petrol's in Kyzyl,' she remarked.

Our conversation continued in this vein for about ten minutes, which is how long it took for another car to pull in. When it halted, my driver hobbled towards the driver, hesitated and, apparently discouraged, gave up on the idea. He hobbled in resignation back to the bench.

'Why doesn't he ask?' Irina queried.

'He's too passive,' I theorised. 'He needs self-assertiveness training.'

'Ruslin! *Perestan!*' she said, growing impatient. 'I suppose he's waiting for his friend to come from Kyzyl.'

With the arrival of several more vehicles, our luck seemed to have changed. A truck pulled in. Irina disappeared from my side, leaving me alone in the car with Ruslin, who had begun playing with the contents of his grandmother's bags. Suddenly a carton of milk plopped open, the contents spilling across the seat.

'Ruslin!' I said, taking out a tissue to wipe it up. '*Perestan!*' But as I said this, something else caught my attention. It was Irina. She hung from the door of the truck, her ankles crossed delicately in the air like a ballet dancer's, working on the truck driver with a seductive smile that showed her teeth in full blossom. The driver shook his head solemnly.

'Ruslin,' I said senselessly. 'You see that truck your grandmother's hanging off over there? It runs on diesel.'

Suddenly, my driver hobbled over grinning wildly. '*Benzin!*' he said. A Russian and his family, taking pity on us, had agreed to donate a litre or two for our cause. My driver took a hose from the boot, stuck it in the Russian's petrol tank and sucked cautiously. Nothing happened. He sucked again, this time more vigorously. Nothing came out. He peered down the hose and into the petrol tank. Then, to the displeasure of our donor's wife and two children, he poked a stick vigorously into the tank.

'*Benzin nyetu?*' he asked our donor.

'*Yest*,' came the reply. There was petrol, apparently, but it didn't seem to want to come out.

My driver scratched his head. 'Do you mind if I run it through the engine?' The Russian reluctantly agreed. Before the Russian could change his mind, my driver unscrewed the petrol hose from the engine and placed it in a container. 'Okay, start the engine!' he called, and with this, petrol began trickling out. One of the Russian children suddenly burst into tears. Ruslin, who had been atoning for the spilt milk with a rare moment of calm, went out in sympathy.

'Ruslin!' his grandmother said, still smarting from the truck driver's rejection. '*Perestan!*'

When Ruslin's shrieks became too much to bear, I got out of the car. I shouldn't have. The commotion had attracted the attention of one of the GAI officers. He looked at me, looked away for a moment, then looked again.

Suddenly it clicked. He moved slowly, menacingly, towards me, rounded the back of the car, sized me up, approached, caught me with a gaze as taut as piano wire and, at the last minute, veered off to where my driver contentedly siphoned off petrol under the bonnet. Still fixing me with the piano-wire stare, the GAI officer lowered his head and quietly asked the driver, 'Eh, is he a foreigner?'

My driver looked up from the bonnet, glanced at me, and replied, 'Yes.'

The officer immediately demanded to see my passport and ordered me to accompany him to the dog box. I acquiesced. He had a Kalashnikov. And he had my passport. Soon, I thought, he might have a few dollars, too.

The interior of the dog box closely resembled the exterior, as if someone had turned it inside out and thrown in a desk and files for decoration. The GAI officer took a seat at the desk, glancing now and then through the window into the yard. I followed his glance and saw my driver, head bowed, still happily pumping out petrol.

'Where have you been?' barked the officer.

'Kyzyl,' I replied.

'Where?'

'Hotel Kyzyl.'

'Stamp?'

'There is no stamp.'

He thought about this for a moment, rifled through the pages of my passport again, shook his head and asked, 'Were you registered.'

'Of course,' I replied. 'But it wasn't stamped.'

'Hotel Kyzyl?' he repeated.

'Yes.'

'No stamp?'

'No.'

He glanced up, perplexed at the activity outside, at Irina in the car, at Ruslin now calmly perched on her lap sucking his thumb, at the concerned Russian family looking on.

'But you *were* registered?' he almost pleaded.

'Sure, sure. I was registered.'

He visibly relaxed and withdrew an old exercise book from the drawer of the desk and began filling in my particulars.

'Sign here, please,' he said. 'You're our first Australian in the book,' he added, and proudly snapped it shut.

I was glad to get out of the GAI office. I was glad to be under way again. I was glad that we had petrol, even if it was only enough to carry us to the next town. The only thing I wasn't glad about was our driver.

'Now!' he said, climbing back into the car. 'See! No problem. *Benzin*.'

I could have killed him, but I decided to smoke a cigarette instead. We pulled out of the parking area just as a truck coughed by in the direction of Kyzyl. Irina, Ruslin and I stared at it in silence. Only the driver seemed not to notice it. It was a petrol tanker.

It took us an hour or so to reach the next town, and the warning light on the petrol gauge flashed for all but ten minutes of that time. Of course, there was not a drop of petrol to be had there, but as luck would have it, two Tuvans had broken down by the roadside and were engaging in repairs.

In all the excitement my driver forgot about his knee again, jumped out and did another spectacular 'triple Tuvan with knee clench and gurgle' across the ground. Dusting himself off, he hobbled over to his countrymen with irrepressible enthusiasm and engaged them in conversation.

'Tuvans!' came the exclamation from our driver when he returned. And as if wishing to make a logical connection, he added, '*Benzin!*'

I wasn't convinced by his Tuvan + Car = Petrol equation, but as it turned out, our Tuvan friends were generous. We had enough to reach the Minusinsk plain. There, the driver assured me, we would find even more petrol.

'How do you know?' I asked.

'Because there was petrol yesterday.'

'And what about all the places back down the road,' I asked. 'Was there petrol there too?'

'No,' he replied.

'But you still didn't fill up in Kyzyl?'

'That was yesterday,' he explained.

I was becoming dangerous.

The Western Sayan Mountains form one of the most beautiful ranges in Russia. Craggy peaks rise to well over 2000 metres, the slopes blanketed in silver fir, cedar and spruce. The valleys contain hidden pristine lakes, home to elk, deer, bears, sable, Siberian weasels and wolves, most of which I'd seen stuffed in Kyzyl's museum. Because the ridges run parallel, seen from the back seat of a Lada, each mountain ridge gives the impression of being the last before the plain. But as we went along, I realised the ridges were getting higher, not lower, and each picturesque valley seemed to exceed the splendid beauty of its predecessor.

The petrol gauge light blinked menacingly near my driver's gammy knee.

'Ruslin! *Perestan!*' Irina shouted.

'Now Abakan!' said the driver, overcome with pleasure. 'Beautiful mountains! Look!'

And then suddenly, climbing over the last ridge, the Minusinsk Plain spread out like a dirty brown blanket before our eyes. Ruslin began to cry again.

The driver killed the engine and we cruised silently down the slopes, re-starting once we'd reached the plain. Little Ruslin stopped crying, climbed over his grandmother's lap and stared out the window at passing cars.

'There!' my driver exclaimed. '*Benzin!*' And sure enough, this time the petrol station was open. Feeling vindicated, my driver pulled up at a pump, whispering to himself *benzin, benzin* as if these two fiery syllables would explain the creation of the Earth, its very reason for being, and cause of its ultimate destruction. I celebrated our success by doing something I didn't usually do at petrol stations. I lit a cigarette. The driver and Irina climbed out, stretched in relief, and set priorities.

'You want something to eat?' Irina asked.

'No,' I replied.

'I do,' my driver said. 'I'll come too.'

'You watch Ruslin, then?'

'I'll watch him,' I assured her.

My companions seemed to take a long time getting the food. After several minutes, Ruslin grew restless, opened the door, and waddled across the yard. He picked up stones and tried to throw them at passing cars; he kicked a rubbish bin, causing its contents to spew across the ground. Then he made off for the mechanic's ramp he'd noticed in the distance and tried to climb its wooden beams from behind. Abandoning that as too difficult, he decided on the easier approach from the sloped ramp. I watched to see he didn't suddenly change his mind and run on the road instead. He struggled up the ramp, at times on all fours, sometimes erratically on twos. I had no idea what he had in mind. He looked back at me to make sure I was watching. I was. Reaching the top, he stood upright and faced the road and passing cars, pulled down his trousers and, arms proudly extended as wings, shot gushes of golden piss onto the dry ground below.

'Ruslin . . . !' a voice cried from the distance.

'Now!' my driver called enthusiastically as he stuck the nozzle into the tank.

A costly trip

Pat Yale

Pat spent several years selling holidays before abandoning sensible careerdom to mix teaching with extensive travel in Europe, Asia, and Central and South America. On one occasion she spent eight months travelling alone across Africa. Now a full-time writer, Pat has worked on Lonely Planet's *Ireland*, *Turkey*, *Britain* and *London* guides. She has lived in London, Cambridge, Cirencester and Bristol, and currently resides in Turkey.

I could tell that something was wrong even before I opened my eyes. The ominous silence surrounding me was broken by a rhythmic swishing sound. For a moment I had no idea where I was. After all, in four months on the road there had been so many different beds.

I snapped open my eyes and hastily closed them again. What they had taken in was just too embarrassing: there I was, lying in solitary splendour on the floor of Nairobi Central Station with no other passengers in sight, just a lone sweeper with his twig broom working his way around the hall and studiously ignoring this single white female spread-eagled on her sleeping bag, her backpack for a pillow.

I glanced at my watch. Six o'clock. Just four hours earlier the scene had been very different when I'd crawled off the night train from Western Kenya with what looked like half of Nairobi. Then, apparently, no-one had had a home to go to. I'd watched my fellow passengers confidently unrolling blankets on the floor and preparing to bed down for the night, and hadn't thought twice about joining them. With mugging a known hazard of visiting Nairobi, arriving post-midnight without a bed to call my own was inviting trouble. How much more sensible to join this embryo squatter city and wait until daylight to brave the streets.

Now, it seemed, I'd slept through the cacophony of a massed departure. It was beyond credulity. Surely nobody could sleep that deeply.

I jumped up and gathered my belongings, averting my eyes from the sweeper. Memories flooded back. Nakuru in the Rift Valley. The flamingos goose-stepping along the shores of the lake. But there had been a hefty price to pay for that glorious sight: a cell-like hotel room where mosquitoes hummed incessantly, defying me to lower my eyelids lest they descend at once and bite. No sleep then, and not much on the rackety old train to Nairobi either.

I stood up, ready to heft my backpack onto my shoulders and exit casually with the air of one who habitually crashes out alone on station floors. But lo and behold a blister had sprouted on my upper arm, a bulging, sulphurous thing just where the strap of my pack should have fitted. I stared at it in disbelief. I knew it hadn't been there yesterday, so where could it have sprung from? Even with two sleepless nights behind me, surely I couldn't have been so comatose as to not feel a passer-by dropping their cigarette end on me?

To put my backpack on properly now would be to risk a messy accident. I cast a sly glance at the sweeper but he had better things to worry about than my antics. I slung my pack over one shoulder and slunk out of the station in search of the Iqbal Hotel.

'Yes, yes, we have a room.' The receptionist at the Iqbal was all smiles. 'Come this way please.'

Up went the backpack over one shoulder again as I set off in pursuit. Up the stairs we went and along a corridor. It was still early, and quite dark once we moved away from the pool of light in the hall.

The receptionist veered to the right. I hurried after him, but in the dim light I failed to see the three steps separating us. Seconds later I was sprawling on the floor once again as the sixteen kilos of my backpack swung down and round to land with a thud on my right wrist.

There followed a fleeting second of false hope. I'd once made the mistake of slamming my finger in an old-fashioned train door. Removing it gingerly, I'd anticipated an instantaneous belt of pain. For a brief instant none came, as the message relayed itself from finger to brain and back again. Then, wham, just as the finger had burst into furious, agonised throbbing, so now my wrist started to shriek with pain.

I picked myself up quickly, gulping back tears. The receptionist rushed to help. 'Are you all right? Let me take your bag,' he said with delightfully mistimed gallantry.

'I'm fine, I'm fine,' I mumbled, like a high-street shopper tripped by a loose paving stone who gathers up the broken eggs and spilt milk whilst simultaneously trying to pull together her shattered dignity and repel those rushing to offer assistance.

Safely in my room, I slumped on the bed, gasping in agony and biting back tears. Pain tore at my wrist and ripped up my arm. The room swam in and out of focus. Never mind, I comforted myself deliriously. Broken bones don't hurt. You must have sprained it.

Where I, a veteran of a St John's Ambulance Brigade first aid unit, had acquired this crazy notion remains a mystery. I closed my eyes and a miraculous gift for sleeping whenever and wherever permitted merciful oblivion to wash over me again.

Half an hour later the receptionist was tapping at the door, full of human concern for his fallen guest. Dredged back from sleep, I registered the dismal fact that the pain hadn't abated one iota.

'I'm fine,' I yelled through the door. A chemist, a chemist, I thought. What I need is an elastic bandage.

Outside, Nairobi was waking up to a new day. Street peddlers were staking out their plots, hawking woven baskets with thick leather straps and a selection of ebony giraffes and heads with elongated earlobes. There was a handy pharmacy nearby. For a few shillings I bought a bandage and wound it tightly round my wrist. The pain eased off and so, at once, did any nagging concern about its source.

In mid-May the heat and humidity of Nairobi was intense; my arm sweated wretchedly beneath its casing. It was hard enough to generate the energy to move away from a fan, even without the dull ache that followed me around. Now I could barely bring myself to move from my bed. The furthest I ventured was to the blissful cool of the British Council library, where even the distraction of the throbbing couldn't prevent my eyes homing in on Rob Papini. Rob was big, tall and clad in baggy white Sudanese trousers perfect for the soggy heat. He wore his glasses suspended on string round his neck like an aged aunt and barely looked up from his book to catch this wreck of a traveller, grubby, dejected and afraid to move her arm, eyeing him surreptitiously over her copy of the *Guardian*.

On day three I pulled myself together to explore the covered market and admire the piles of tropical fruit interspersed with yet more ebony giraffes and outsize earlobes. It was late in the day before I made it back to the Iqbal and there, in the café, sat Rob, staring into space over a cup of brick-red tea.

On autopilot I steered my way to his table and sat down. He eyed me warily but lust had washed away my inhibitions. Unfortunately, I couldn't pick up a cup or wield a knife. Nor was it easy to fancy myself a *femme fatale* with one arm swaddled like a mummy. We shared a bottle of wine which set woozy romantic fantasies racing round my brain. Rob had mastered the Jarvis Cocker trick of managing to look both nerdily old-fashioned and coolly trendy at the same time. Staring into his alluringly myopic eyes had the soothing effect that two days of bed rest had so singularly failed to produce. Thus it was that I forgot to use my left hand when picking up a glass to toast our trip. The gasp of pain provoked by this simple mistake was enough to bring me crashing back to earth.

'Are you sure it's just sprained?' Rob ventured. 'Maybe it's broken.'

Gloomily I unwrapped the wrist. Thick weals of purple glowered up at me.

'Ahhh,' was all I could think of to say.

The next morning I decided to do what I should have done on day one and seek expert opinion. A bus trundling along the high street had 'Kenyatta Hospital' on the front, so I hopped aboard.

The hospital was set in rolling grassland on a hillside on the outskirts of town. Casualty was as jammed to overflowing as on any Saturday night at home and I joined a miserable line-up of cuts, bruises and broken bones. A nurse in crisp white uniform took down my name; it was all comfortingly familiar. Only one detail jolted me into remembering just how many thousands of miles away from the National Health Service I actually was: two hefty men stood by the door armed with batons to ward off would-be queue-jumpers.

An Indian doctor inspected my wrist, tut-tutted at the weals, X-rayed it and confirmed what by now was blindingly obvious – I'd fractured it in the fall. Off I went to the plaster-cast department to be moulded into rigidity. The doctor grinned at me. 'Come back in three weeks,' he laughed. 'Keep your arm steady. Don't do anything like this,' and he wiggled his own arm up and down in the air in imitation of some weird sexual perversion or the more mundane battering likely to be endured by a traveller on one of Kenya's back roads.

Waiting for the bus back to town with my right arm strapped across my chest, I met a diminutive, fine-framed young man with his left arm strapped across his chest and a lugubrious expression plastered onto his face. 'I'm a jockey for the Kenya Jockey Club,' he answered my dutiful query. 'My horse threw me.'

'Will it be all right?' I asked, knowing even less about jockeying than I did about broken bones.

'I don't know.' His expression grew yet more cloudy. 'If it isn't, I won't be able to work again.'

I'd been worrying that my plans to visit the paradisc island of Lamu would have to be put on ice in accordance with the doctor's injunction. But Jani's plight was real, mine mere play acting. I mumbled the sort of pointless pleasantries such situations seem to demand: it'll be all right, I'm sure you'll be riding again in weeks – these from a woman who had self-diagnosed her own broken wrist as a sprain.

We rattled back to town, holding our defective limbs as stiffly still as we could while keeping a wary eye out for pickpockets. 'Let's go for lunch,' I suggested, and we headed for a café which would suit his normal budget and my skinflint backpacker's one.

Kenya's national dish is a big football of cassava topped off with a smattering of sauce, perhaps with a mouthful or two of meat. Difficult enough to carve with two good arms, this delicacy became a slippery eel of impossibility with just one. Between us, however, Jani and I had two useable limbs and between us we struggled through the meal while he told me about life as a jockey. In a town where most men struggled to find work that paid anything at all, Jani earned an excellent wage. No wonder he looked so wretched at the prospect of having it snatched away by a fall.

There's not much a right-handed person can do to entertain herself in a strange country when the arm on which she depends has been rendered useless. It wasn't just the difficulty of washing, dressing and hauling myself in and out of buses. Try as I might to expel such thoughts from my mind, fear of attack dogged my footsteps. One by one, able-bodied travellers would return to the Iqbal with tales of woe. How could my plastered arm not mark me out as an easy victim? I fretted, even though the cast would make an excellent weapon with which to bash anyone foolish enough to grab me.

Rob and I moved into a room together, and spent long hours smoking dubious substances and comparing notes on our past lives. He had spent the previous year teaching in Sudan and was toying with conversion to Islam. 'When I get back to England,' he told me earnestly, 'I think I'll tell my girlfriend we can't resume our sexual relationship.'

'But what if she wants to?' I asked gloomily, beating back the urge to ask, 'And what if I want to sleep with you now?'

'I hadn't thought of that,' Rob replied and lapsed into stoned silence.

Our cosy, exclusive bubble of intimacy was soon burst when a middle-aged Indian moved into the vacant third bed. He lay there sweating and moaning. 'Malaria,' said Rob. 'Plague,' said the friend who occasionally turned up to minister to him.

'Is plague infectious?' I asked Rob.

'No idea,' he shrugged and we smoked another joint.

Eventually I could no longer bear Nairobi and the frustration of being so close to someone so blind to my feelings. The train to Mombasa sounded smooth-running enough to satisfy even the fiercest of doctors. One evening I waved a sad goodbye to Rob and took the train to the coast, treating myself to second class and the luxury of a soft, velvety couchette. Evening raced into night with a glorious sunburst of orange and red, and in the morning the lumbering figures of elephants trundled past in slow motion as we transited the Tsavo National Park.

But the muggers, it seemed, had followed me to Mombasa. 'Don't walk on this beach,' people would say. 'Don't walk on that one.'

Desperate now, I bused north to Malindi, smaller, quieter and seemingly safe. But the beach hang-outs crawled with ex-pats with a fine line in negativity. 'Where did you get your arm set?' they would ask, before rattling off a list of private hospitals whose existence I hadn't even considered. When I demurred and told them I'd gone to the Kenyatta, their faces would twist alarmingly. 'Oh dear, you shouldn't have gone there,' they would intone. 'Of course it won't be set properly. You'll have to have it broken and reset when you go back.'

In the evening the crabs came to a circular café on the beach, waving their pincers and scuttling sideways to evade the feet that kicked them. I felt for them and for myself, hating the ex-pats for their knee-jerk cruelty and racism. Alone on the beach, I peered up at the sky and picked out the Southern Cross, a symbol of how far I was from home. Phil Collins played on the jukebox, a tear-jerking song of loneliness and longing. A wave of homesickness sloshed over me. I retreated to my thatched hut and wept for the loss of Rob.

Two weeks had passed since my fall. The plaster continued to itch and sweat but the pain had ebbed to an occasional twinge. I craved for Lamu as only a hardened backpacker cooped up in a package-holidaymakers' enclave can crave for escape. On the map it didn't look so far from Malindi, but the road's confident black line gradually petered out into a line of dots, which could only mean dirt track with bumps. The travellers' grapevine ran hot with rumours of Somali attacks on the buses.

My nice Indian doctor would have had a heart attack had he glimpsed the vehicle into which I finally carried my wrist. Battered and broken, it looked as if it had just arrived from a war zone. 'Filthy' would have been a generous way to describe its interior. Mud streaked the floor and windows, and the seats were secured to the luggage-rack with pieces of string.

The one saving grace was that so many people finally boarded the bus that it was hard to move at all, let alone jolt up and down. I sat surrounded by women in gaily coloured *kangas*, their babies fastened to their backs with matching wraps, and by men in tattered relics of once-smart shirts and trousers. No-one talked much. It was enough to hold on and endure.

The road was reasonable as far north as Garsen, whereupon it crumbled abruptly into sticky red mud. We emptied out of the bus for lunch in a dismal frontier settlement where there were clues, had I known how to read them, as to what was happening elsewhere in Africa. Scattered amongst the sturdy, stubby Kenyan men were tall, willowy Somali cattle herders whose long tartan skirts left their upper bodies exposed. To observe the lack of flesh on their chests was bad enough, but to see the wasted bodies of their treasured cattle was to weep: the skin had fallen away so completely that their ribcages stood out like bars. But they were the lucky ones. By the roadside lay the carcasses of those who could stumble no further. It was 1984 and famine was marching its way across the Sahel.

By the time we reached Lamu my body was almost as rigid as my arm. I peeled myself off the seat, checked for further broken limbs, and marched off to discover the sweetest little hotel in Africa, its mosquito net suspended over the bed like a bridal veil.

Lamu was everything I'd dreamed it would be. Here were not just the beaches of fine coral sand, the limpid blue sea and wavering coconut palms of Malindi, but gorgeous old stone houses with carved wooden doorways, the northern flowering of the Swahili architecture that blossomed so brightly in Zanzibar's Stone Town. There were no cars on the island, and the dhow-builders still passed their days knocking up shark-finned boats that tacked their way up and down the coast. The high-rise hotels of Malindi, with their pampered, Kenyan-hating clientele, were blotted out as if they'd never existed.

Of course, still touting my plaster, I could only gaze at the waves with the same thwarted yearning as I'd gazed at Rob in Nairobi. But just as the air had dried out as the bus headed north, so the rivulets of sweat had at last stopped rolling from under my cast. Nor did I need to worry about wielding my arm in self-defence any more. All was right with my world. And then I walked along the promenade and saw Rob emerging from a hotel.

We adjourned to a café and tucked into those travellers' staples: milkshakes and banana pancakes. Maybe I'd known he was coming after me and maybe I hadn't. He looked just as outlandish here in his Sudanese clothes, just as desirable, just as remote and unattainable. We picked up where we'd left off at the Iqbal, talking into the small hours, reading, smoking, close, close, close – yet never quite close enough for me.

I could have stayed on Lamu for ever had there been a hospital. We toyed with hacking my arm free of its casing with a Swiss army knife but the words of those wretched Malindi ex-pats had planted their poisonous seeds. I planned a career as a writer. How would that pan out if my all-important right wrist really had been badly set? There was little alternative but to return to Nairobi.

A storm came suddenly in great bursts of thunder and lightning, raining coconuts onto the beach, drenching the sands and bleaching the landscape. I boarded the bus back to Nairobi with a heavy heart, for Rob was heading south for Zanzibar and Zimbabwe. Our paths might never cross again. I prayed that he would commit himself to a rendezvous, but we were British and reserved, and kissed good-bye like a pair of elderly cousins. 'See you,' I said miserably, and that was that.

The threat from the Somali raiders had increased, and soldiers with machine guns occupied the back seat of the bus to ensure our safety. This bus was no cleaner or newer than the last, but at least it was relatively empty. After two hours I turned to look at the guards. They were sleeping with their heads resting on each other's shoulders like babies.

The rain had worked terrible tricks on the road surface, churning it to the consistency of a motorcycle circuit after a hard day's scrambling. The bus slithered and slipped, bounced over ridges, dipped down into muddy puddles. Then suddenly, without warning, it skidded across the road and came to rest with its back wheels wedged in a ditch. The crunch jolted the soldiers awake and they shot to their feet, snatching up their guns and looking around wildly. With long-suffering sighs, the passengers stumbled to their feet and headed for the exit.

We stood in silence, inspecting the damage. If the bus had looked forlorn before, now it looked beyond hope of deliverance. The soldiers arrayed themselves at each end, guns pointed down the road to repel any raider hoping to cash in on our misfortune. The driver produced a rope and tied it to the front bumper. The men lined up and tugged. The bus heaved momentarily forwards, then groaned and slipped back even further into the ditch. Another rope was produced and tied to its rear end. Now the passengers were divided into two groups. I, of course, could do nothing but cheer helplessly from the sideline as the tug-of-war teams hauled on their ropes.

Slipping and sliding in the gruesome mud, the men could barely stand up, let alone exert enough muscle power to move the bus. But, egged on by the soldiers with hearty yells, they tried and tried again until at last their efforts were rewarded. The bus surged forward, paused as if considering a retreat, and then leapt back onto the road. A great roar of relief was raised. The soldiers slapped each other on the back and lowered their guns. Congratulating each other with the false heartiness of those who were more frightened than they'd cared to let on, the passengers clambered back into the bus and slumped down into their seats. Five minutes later I eyed the back seat. Our guards were fast asleep once again.

Back at the Kenyatta, my Indian doctor had lost none of his good cheer. 'You're fine,' he assured me. 'Nothing to worry about. Just go and get this plaster removed.'

I shuffled down the corridor and into a room where a small boy was having the plaster sliced off his leg with a circular saw. He was stoical about the buzzing, and totally unfazed as bits of cast flew around him. I, on the other hand, averted my eyes when it was my turn. The nurse roared with laughter at this proof of the cowardice of the *muzungus*.

By now I'd been in Kenya for six weeks and it was long past time to move on. Also staying at the Iqbal was Helen, a New Zealander who had forfeited her passport to a mugger. We decided to join forces and head for Zanzibar, where I tried not to bank on rediscovering Rob. Now that the cast had been removed, my arm was striped white and brown, but for the first time in weeks I was squeaky clean and almost human. Perhaps now, I dreamed, he would see me as I saw him: as a consummate object of desire.

Before leaving, I took Jani out for one last football of cassava. His wrist was also out of plaster and we laughed over the idiocy of the ex-pats. My writing arm was fine. He, too, was confident of being back in the saddle soon.

On Zanzibar I found Rob again, sure enough, but it was no different. We were friends, good friends, and nothing more. He wrote me one final letter from Zimbabwe: 'I'll be home in July. Looking forward to seeing you. We'll have so much to talk about.'

I never heard from him again.

Watch your step

Brad Wong

Brad is a freelance writer, currently studying Chinese in Beijing. He was most recently a reporter for the *Pacific Daily News* on Guam and has covered politics, illegal immigration and the Asian economic crisis. His work has appeared in the *Salinas Californian*, *San Jose Mercury News*, the *Congressional Quarterly Weekly Report* and *Asian Week*. Brad has completed a 2000-kilometre solo mountain-bike trek from Beijing to Hunan province.

WE had been travelling for more than ten hours through central China's lush countryside, and were somewhere between the cities of Xi'an and Luoyang. Gas fumes permeated the crowded bus, making me nauseous. I wanted my day's journey to end.

I was travelling with a group of Chinese college professors and students on a weekend trip to the temple where Chinese Buddhism began, taking in some nearby Buddhist caves and the birthplace of Chinese martial arts along the way.

At around midnight, the bus driver pulled over to a roadside latrine to let his passengers 'use the facilities' – a few brick walls near a field of vegetables. I stumbled off to stretch my legs, breathe the fresh country air and enjoy the relaxing evening; I also wanted to find a quiet corner where I could relieve myself.

Several women ducked behind the latrine's wall, while the men stood on the edge of the field, away from the headlights of the bus.

As an American I wanted privacy, and I wandered around until I spotted the latrine's back wall. The isolated area seemed like the perfect place. As I walked toward it, fatigued from the day's long and bouncy bus trip and the nauseous fumes, I stared dazedly at the wall's faint outline in the moonlight.

Within seconds I heard a splash, and found myself walking through a shallow pond. One whiff of the stench snapped me out of my stupor. My brain instantly fired off a message: 'Don't dwell on the details here, but something is wrong with this picture.'

'Do you know what happened?' I asked a colleague in loud, exasperated tones as I climbed out of the hole. 'Do you know what happened?'

She did – and so did the other passengers. When you're the only person to tumble into a Chinese countryside latrine on a clear, quiet evening and climb out yelling in English, people just know.

As news spread throughout the group, my fellow passengers fired a cacophony of unanswerable questions, as though they were my know-it-all relatives.

'Why didn't you see the hole?'

'How could you do a thing like that?'

'Don't stand there. Stand over there. Watch out! Women are going to the bathroom over there.'

I think it was their way of showing they cared about my safety, even though their comments couldn't reverse my plunge and remove my newly acquired scent.

They probably wondered how I, a Westerner, could survive travelling in the world's most-populous country. I mean, if I couldn't stay out of a Chinese countryside toilet at night when they were with me, what could happen when they weren't around to look out for me?

I grabbed my backpack from the bus and searched for any article of dry and clean clothing I could find. I finally found my long underwear, a pair of shorts and my river-rafting sandals.

By then, the college official responsible for the group's safety was standing next to me. 'Why didn't you go to the bathroom like the rest of the men?' he yelled at me, as I peeled off my pants and threw a wet sock on the ground.

The other men were by the side of the road – facing the field. That's where it was safe and dry. He kept pointing at them.

I understood his concern. When the Chinese go on group tours, one person is often responsible for everyone's safety. And with three Chinese Americans as guests on this tour, he had to make sure that he protected our safety at all costs.

I put my boots, socks and pants into a plastic bag and approached the bus, not caring where I dumped my clothing. I just wanted the night to be over. But the driver cared, hastily stowing my bag in an outside compartment.

When I boarded the bus, the passengers continued to stare and whisper among themselves. As I walked down the bus aisle looking for a seat, I was like Moses, parting a sea of Chinese students and professors on my left and right. 'They're talking about you,' my friend whispered to me.

I suspected that. But again, what could I say? It would have been pointless to say what all travellers who want to smooth over an awkward or embarrassing situation say to locals: 'Your country is so beautiful! It has a long history! The food is so delicious! The people are so friendly! I think I'll return next year!'

It was dark. I was woozy. I missed a step. There was no use getting upset.

There was one positive outcome: my fellow passengers learned some new English words to describe what happened. A Chinese American friend, who taught English at the college, discussed bodily gases, fluids and solids – and the Western street language used to explain what the body rejects.

Having changed my clothing, I had hoped that I would smell better. But as I took that long walk down the bus aisle in search of a place to sit, a young woman sitting next to an empty seat looked up and politely said, 'This seat has a person.'

It didn't, so I sat down. But for the rest of the trip, I slid my hands under my thighs and tried to keep my feet and legs away from nearby passengers. For the first time in my life, I was glad that several men on the bus were puffing on cigarettes, the smoke lingering in the air above our heads in the cabin.

So, if you ever visit China, please heed this advice: watch your step. The country is different in many ways. It has some spectacular scenery, a 5000-year history and the Great Wall. It also has some big holes in the ground.

And if your long-distance bus pulls over for a midnight toilet stop, do what I should have done: follow the locals very closely. You may also want to carry some cologne or perfume. It may help.

Expulsion from Hanoi

Daniel Robinson

Daniel was raised in the USA (the San Francisco Bay Area and Glen Ellyn, Illinois) and Israel. His first trip, at age seventeen, was to Cyprus, and since then he has spent several years backpacking around Asia, parts of the Middle East and Europe. His work for Lonely Planet includes the first edition of *Vietnam, Laos & Cambodia* and all three editions of the *France* guide. Daniel completed a BA in Near Eastern Studies at Princeton University in 1990 and lives in Tel Aviv with his wife, Yael Arami.

AFTER a decade of tourism and increasing economic openness, Hanoi is known to legions of travellers as a delicate, highly cultured city of ancient temples, bustling markets, lakeside parks and French colonial architecture. The image of Hanoi as the inaccessible capital of a secretive communist state, ruled by commissars and secret police, a place where dissidents disappear into a network of labour camps – all this now seems almost as far away as the last French governor-general.

In the late 1980s, however – when 'capitalist tourists' were virtually unknown in Vietnam, the USSR was still a super-power and *doi moi* (Vietnam's version of perestroika) was still gestating – the place seemed to run according to rules, codes and assumptions unlike those I'd ever encountered in all my travels. It seemed natural to think of the country as being totally separate from the rest of Asia, almost in another dimension or from a different era: somewhere you flew 'into' and 'out of' rather than 'to' and 'from'. When you were in Vietnam, you were very, very far from anywhere else, isolated not only by the paucity of flights but also by the atmosphere of fear and weariness that permeated every aspect of life. And nowhere did life feel as regulated, regimented and unfree – and nowhere did the visitor feel as watched – as in Hanoi.

I, too, was not without apprehension, and as my notes for the first edition of *Vietnam: a travel survival kit* became more and more voluminous – and valuable, representing many weeks of sixteen-hour days – I became more and more fearful that they would be seized. I was not concerned for my physical safety – it was unthinkable that my actual person would be violated – but a guidebook writer pours their heart and soul into their research, ferreting out bits of practical, historical and cultural detail that may some day, for someone, make the difference between a delightful outing and a logistical nightmare. 'What if they seize my notes?' I kept asking myself. I had images of being stopped at the airport when leaving the country and finding myself flying towards Bangkok without my precious scribblings. As often as possible I tracked down photocopy machines and copied my notes, sending them out of the country in batches with Western tourists.

The words 'totalitarian police state' conjure up images of efficient, ruthless officials who follow all directives with thoroughness and precision. But when policies change and rumours of openness are afloat, it's not always clear, even to officialdom itself, where the boundaries lie. At the time, the cadres running Vietnam hardly knew what a tourist was and had even less of a clue about what a travel guidebook might be; as a result, a guidebook writer was a totally unknown life form. It was unclear to everyone, including the people running the government tourism apparatus, what, exactly, was permitted to someone like me. For instance, did I need internal travel permits, and if so, when? In later years, all tourists would be required to carry internal visas, usually available for a small fee or a slightly larger bribe, but back before there was even a guidebook, policy had yet to be spelled out.

All around I saw signs of halting but significant change, some of them unexpected and even bizarre. In the Central Highlands town of Dalat, for instance, word on the streets had it that anyone who could produce the body of a missing American serviceman would get to go to America. Other rumours spoke of large amounts of cash on offer for dead GIs. I was one of the first Americans anyone had seen in Dalat in a very long time, and so it was to me that gruesome proposals were made. All I could do was refer these local 'entrepreneurs' to the American MIA team then combing the country for remains. I knew, too, that the human remains in question almost certainly belonged to one of the hundreds of thousands of Vietnamese MIAs, perhaps passed off to a local 'investor' by an unscrupulous wheeler-dealer who had salted a pile of bone fragments with a US Army dog tag to make it look authentic. I thought of the families in the States who had been waiting for twenty or more years to hear of their loved ones' fate, but was well aware that I was in no position to ease their pain. Anyone with 'goods' to sell would, sooner or later, make contact with the proper authorities and, more likely than not, discover that the 'next egg' they'd put away as a long-term investment – in the finest capitalist tradition of speculation – had no market value.

Some things seemed frozen in time, though. While part of a humanitarian aid delegation (which I was asked to leave when my note-taking raised too many official eyebrows), my colleagues and I mentioned to our Foreign Ministry guide that it seemed strange that we were always assigned the exact same room in each hotel. Were we being bugged everywhere we went? Preposterous, he said, smiling mischievously: Vietnam is a poor country and we don't have nearly enough bugging equipment to mount so many wiretapping operations. But in our rooms we still wrote notes (rather than speaking) to the few, very nervous Vietnamese friends who dropped by to visit, and the head of the delegation would let her mentally handicapped teenage son wander the city alone, on the assumption that if he got lost or into some sort of trouble the police minders keeping an eye on all of us would be there to help. It was a very convenient set-up: Vietnam's secret police as mobile, 24-hour-a-day child minders, provided free of charge to foreign guests of suspect nationality.

As I neared the end of my research, one major information-gathering operation remained: travelling overland from Saigon to Hanoi for a second time. I had run into a few travellers who had done the trip solo with permits issued in Hanoi, but when I tried to get the necessary internal visas in Saigon officialdom refused. Apparently, the request was unprecedented. But perhaps I didn't really need all that paperwork, a tourism official suggested. 'We can't give you the permits, but you might just hop on a bus and head north.' The choice was simple: either produce a pretty pathetic guidebook or push the envelope.

The gamble seemed to pay off. For three weeks I travelled steadily northward, spending a night or two in each coastal town before once again hitting the road. Using decades-old maps published by the French in the 1920s and by American oil companies in the early 1960s, I sketched updated maps of places such as Qui Nhon and Quang Ngai. Many of the street names had been changed several times: Vietnamese nationalist patriots favoured by Hanoi had replaced other patriots favoured by the former South Vietnamese government, which itself had replaced most of the French colonial names.

Local tourism officials and people's committee representatives were unfailingly cooperative and never once asked to see my papers. Apparently, it was almost unthinkable that I had arrived in their bit of territory without the proper authorisation. The secret police also kept their distance, and the one time they dropped by my hotel room – at 1 am – I showed them my California drivers' licence and they went away. My assurance that I'd be leaving town the next morning seemed to placate them: in a few hours I'd be someone else's problem.

My slow trek northward, mainly by bus and train, was timed so I'd arrive in the impoverished city of Vinh in time to participate in the ground-breaking ceremony for a new children's wing to be added to the local hospital. The project was sponsored by a group of American war veterans, some of whom had come to Vietnam themselves to spend several weeks building the structure alongside their former foes, veterans of the North Vietnamese Army.

After the ceremony, I joined the aid delegation in an old Russian-built bus for the long journey to Hanoi along Highway 1. The bus was soon stopped by the side of the road, its Soviet engine unequal to the task. After a long wait we got moving again, only to halt a while later. I became mildly alarmed when I heard the driver mutter angrily, '*Lien Xo numba ten,*' thinking he was upset at us (as white folk, we were often assumed to be '*Lien Xo*' – Soviets – by the locals). But he was in fact cursing Vietnam's socialist brothers in the USSR, whose barter deals for Vietnamese commodities left the country with the poorest-quality industrial goods the Soviet Union was capable of producing, the ones no-one else in Comecon would take.

After hours of waiting, the broken-down bus was replaced by a functioning one that rolled into Hanoi at about 2 am. The delegation's Foreign Ministry guide offered to put me up at the prestigious Foreign Ministry Guest House in central Hanoi, usually reserved for foreign dignitaries of the highest rank. He promised to arrange a room for US$26, but such a princely sum was way beyond my budget, and from previous visits to Hanoi I knew of hotels that cost just US$6. I got off the bus near the railway station, deserted at that hour, and walked to the nearby Dong Loi Hotel. Banging on the locked front door produced no tangible result, and yet more banging elicited angry refusals to open the door. Foiled in my efforts to get into the hotel, I walked across the street to the police station, where the clerks on duty let me nap on a hard wooden table until morning.

For the first few days I was oblivious to what Hanoi officialdom was cooking up. When asked how I had gotten to Hanoi I answered, truthfully, that I'd come overland from Saigon. Assuming that I was being followed everywhere I went and that reams of information about me were being assembled in a giant dossier, I had long before concluded that openness and complete honesty were my best cover. I was still unsuspecting when I was asked to turn over my passport, and continued to go about my business of gathering logistical information. My new guide (whom Vietnam Tourism had persuaded me to hire, along with a car and a driver – a neat device for separating Westerners from their dollars) was distinctly lacking in enthusiasm, and he clearly had not been given this assignment in recognition of superior linguistic skills.

The next day, as requested, I stopped by the Immigration Police office at 2 pm to 'answer a few questions' and pick up my passport. Over the next two hours I was repeatedly accused of being unable to prove that I had not violated internal travel permit regulations. At the time, the rules on such matters were far from clear-cut, and my visa status (I was not a tourist but rather had been sponsored by Vietnam Tourism, the government tourism authority) made things even murkier. The interrogation ended with a promise that I could pick up my passport the next morning at 10 am. But when I stopped by and paid a fine for violating my permit, instead of my passport I was given a new promise: tomorrow at 9 am your passport will be returned. The fish was being reeled in, gently and stealthily.

I had to admit that the trap was well laid: my guide, in fact a secret-police minder, did his job well, and when I was arrested the next morning absolutely no-one knew I was being held. I am naturally loquacious, and in an effort to be both candid and affable I had provided my captors with enough information for them to know that no-one would miss me if I suddenly disappeared. My planned research trip to Haiphong and Halong Bay, for which I had signed a contract after tough negotiations (all part of the elaborate ruse), turned into a very short drive to the Immigration Police office, where I was read an expulsion order. My Vietnam Tourism 'guide' disappeared, and I was left with three guards. I was under arrest in a city with no US diplomatic presence.

The night before being picked up I had spent several hours sipping beers at the Australian Embassy, exchanging stories and information with diplomats and NGO officials at the weekly Billabong Club. A congenial social affair in the best Australian tradition, the highly informal get-together gave me a chance to find out a bit about Hanoi's expat community. Now, as I sat under police guard, I demanded to see an Australian diplomat, and even contemplated making a run for it – after all, the Australian Embassy was only two blocks north, and I envisioned myself barely outpacing the police as I jumped through the embassy gate. But this course of action seemed risky, to say the least, and chances were I'd be captured within seconds, finding myself in an immeasurably worse position. So I kept repeating, like a mantra, my demand to be allowed to contact an Aussie diplomat, a tactic which seemed only to infuriate police officials.

A request that I be allowed to contact the North American section of the Vietnamese Foreign Ministry was also turned down. It later became clear that my arrest was part of a power play by the hard-line Interior Ministry against the *doi moi* supporters over at the Foreign Ministry. If only I'd spent that first night at the Foreign Ministry Guest House – I'd have been under FM protection and thus virtually untouchable. For the sake of twenty bucks I had forsaken the most valuable patronage a foreign visitor could possibly receive.

At one point, a high-ranking official came into the room and screamed at me, shaking his fists in fury. I had never seen the man before, nor had I ever seen a Vietnamese lose his temper: in East Asia, as the guidebooks never tire of explaining, you yourself lose face if you lose your temper. It was quite obvious that this fellow was really, really furious. A policeman who spoke English threatened that if I did not 'cooperate' I would be held until an American diplomat came from Bangkok to pick me up. 'Cooperating' seemed to consist of my refraining from demanding to see a diplomat, but I knew that unless *someone* knew I was being held, the police officials, already hostile, would be free to do anything they chose. Uppermost in my mind were my notes (including all my notes from Cambodia) and my film. What if they decided to confiscate everything? My mind raced as I tried to figure out some way to save the last two months of intensive, exhausting field research.

After a couple of hours, half a dozen or so policemen came into the room where I was being held and put a U-shaped steel bar around each of my wrists; the two bars were then attached to each other with a steel pin, which was locked in place. Almost immediately, the manacles began to dig into my wrists, cutting off blood circulation. I had seen such handcuffs only once before, among the torture instruments on display at the genocide museum in Phnom Penh. Then the police took away my glasses, leaving me surrounded by a blurry world of indistinct shapes and incomprehensible voices.

A short time later I was marched out of the police office and loaded into a tiny cage in the back of a jeep. As I left the office, I screamed 'Help!! Help!!' at the top of my lungs. What else could I have done? 'Help' seemed so conventional, so unimaginative, but it was brief, to the point and loud enough to cause a commotion. Alas, no foreigners heard or saw me, so far as I know: I was still being held incommunicado, except now I was being driven out of the city in an exhaust-fume filled cage to an unknown destination.

One advantage of being arrested after you've researched a travel guidebook is that you're pretty aware of the geography of your surroundings. And as far as I could tell, the jeep was heading in the general direction of Noi Bai Airport. Before we got there, the jeep turned off onto a side rode and we drove to an isolated police compound. I was left locked in the sweltering cage for about an hour and a half, still manacled and still without glasses. When I was finally let out and taken to a second-floor room for a 'customs check', the handcuffs were finally removed, but some time passed before the numbness in my hands went away and I was able to fill out the forms I was given.

My backpacks were emptied on the table and eight customs officials and policemen began going through everything. My personal letters and diaries were read, my notes examined page by page, and the names of the Vietnamese who had worked with me or whom I'd met were copied down. The customs officials demanded that I turn over my film, promising to process it and return it to me. They had good reason to believe I was something of a sucker, but did they really think I was *that* gullible?! All the while I kept thinking to myself: 'You can write a guidebook without photos but not without notes, so try to throw them off.' I formulated a plan: fight like hell to save the film and pretend that the notes were of little consequence. Even as the policemen were about to discover my 1:10,000-scale military map of Dalat (dated 1962, but still potentially incriminating), I remained impassive, and the bored officer passed right over it.

The 'customs search' ended and I was driven in the jeep to the airport terminal. Finally I'll run into other Westerners and my isolation will end, I thought to myself. And indeed, in the drab terminal building I managed to catch the attention of some of the foreign passengers, several of whom I had met previously. It was at this point that I realised the pre-flight X-raying of my luggage was to be central to officialdom's final assault. In the guise of 'standard procedure' (they had just gone through every single item I owned!), my film would be loaded into the ancient Soviet X-ray machine and fried. In a last act of resistance, I filled my pockets with film canisters before handing over the packs. As soon as the other passengers were herded out of the terminal, four uniformed thugs grabbed me, forced me to the ground and held me in a double half-nelson. I struggled to hold on to my film, but all fourteen rolls of slides – all the photos I'd take in the course of ten weeks of work in Vietnam and Cambodia – were thrown into the antiquated, overpowered gadget and given the full treatment.

All the while, the Thai International flight to Bangkok, which I had been forced to pay for (don't expellees at least get free flights?!), was being held up just for me. Furious at my treatment and outraged by my impotence, I refused to walk and had to be carried out to the jeep, which then drove me out to the aircraft as if I were a VIP. I mounted the gangway, hugely relieved that my notes were still with me, and at the top gave the finger to the cops below, shouting (in Hebrew), 'Fascists!! Fascists!!' The Thai crew tried to calm me as the plane taxied along the runway and took off, soaring above the rice fields still pocked with thousands of water-filled craters made by American bombs, craters that the resourceful Vietnamese had turned into fish ponds.

A close call in the Cooks

David Harcombe

Born in England, David worked as a fundraiser for a large British-based overseas aid charity. After brief visits to Eastern Europe and West Africa, he was lured eastwards through Asia to Australia. After a spell in the Caribbean, Latin America and Southern Africa, he returned to Australia to live in its remote north-western bush, working among Aboriginal Australians. The author of the first two editions of Lonely Planet's *Solomon Islands* and the first edition of *Vanuatu*, David currently lectures in Travel Industry Management studies at a large international university in Bangkok.

T was on my first day in Rarotonga, the main island of the Cook Islands group in the south-east Pacific, that I saw Jeff. I had not seen him for several years, and had no idea he was living there.

He told me that he was teaching on Aitutaki, the Cooks' second most important island, and one of the world's largest coral atolls. I immediately accepted his invitation to visit him over the next few days.

On my arrival at Aitutaki's small airport, I was greeted with a welcoming garland of frangipani flowers placed around my neck by Jean, Jeff's Cook Islander wife. She explained that this was a traditional islander welcome for visitors to their atoll.

Jeff was keen to take me sailing on the atoll's huge lagoon in one of his two new catamarans. While recounting all the many things that fascinated him about the Cooks, he mentioned that he had recently had a small walk-on part in a local movie about a young island boy who had somehow tamed a tiger shark.

I was aware that non-aggressive relationships between individual humans and certain sharks sometimes occurred in the Pacific. But I did not feel very reassured when I learnt that the shark, once the film-making was complete, had been released into Aitutaki's lagoon.

After Jean's welcoming midday meal, it was sailing time. Our other passenger was Mike Woods, a New Zealander who owned a large hotel on Rarotonga, and who also ran several successful tourism operations in Aitutaki.

Jeff was keen to enter the tourism business through his catamarans. It seemed that our sailing trip was not just a welcome for me, but was also intended to impress Mike with Jeff's seamanship as the owner of a potentially prosperous new tourism business.

To give the slender craft speed and balance, Jeff strapped me into what he called its jury-rig. A harness near the mast, it held me suspended halfway over the catamaran's port, or left-hand, side. Although it felt rather uncomfortable, the device certainly seemed to allow our boat to reach impressive speeds.

Mike was crouched at the front, watching the atolls' multitude of tiny islands flash by as we raced down the lagoon. Jeff turned from the tiller and whispered to me, 'Mike's very big in the tourism business here. If he gives me a regular contract, I'm made!'

We were now about one or two kilometres from our intended turning point at the base of the immense lagoon. Suddenly, there was a very loud crack. The catamaran's left-hand hull, just below me and my harness, had buckled.

The now-wounded craft's left-hand hull began to plough deep into the water, listing worryingly on my side. Suddenly, the mast snapped, bringing down the sail in a confusing muddle of cumbersome canvas on top of both Jeff and Mike.

I released myself from the harness, and was preparing to join Jeff at the stern when my camouflage-patterned baseball cap fell into the water. Although the boat at first seemed to be almost stationary, my cap quickly floated out of reach.

It was a hot afternoon. Not only did I need all the protection I could get from the strong sun above, but I was also very fond of my cap. It had been in many exotic places in the Pacific with me, and I could not bear to lose it.

I dived in fully clothed, and quickly retrieved it. But as I turned to swim back to the boat, I discovered I didn't have the energy to catch up with the drifting craft. The tide was too strong. It slowly drew the damaged catamaran away from me, while my water-sodden clothes seemed to anchor me to that one single spot in the ocean.

'Swim, David! Swim!' I could hear Jeff calling out desperately to me.

I tried. I tried so very hard, but I just didn't have the speed to catch up with the damaged boat, as the tide drew it steadily away.

Just as with all those cliches about mortal danger at sea, my thinking became crystal-clear. I had to stay with the boat if I were to survive.

I knew that there was a thick nylon fishing line trailing behind our craft, with a huge triple-barbed hook on its end. I had to grab that line and haul myself in, hopefully not snagging myself on the sharp hook at the same time.

As I reached desperately for the nylon life-line, I saw some low-lying palm-covered islands in the distance. I wondered if I could reach them, if I missed the line. They seemed so far away, even though the distance was probably only a couple of kilometres. And if I actually reached them, would I be able to climb any of the trees to get at the coconuts, both for food and water, until rescue came?

Alternatively, would my slow, exhausted progress to those distant islands attract the tiger shark's attention? For all I knew, it might be in the water behind me even now. All these thoughts crossed my mind as I lunged for the life-saving fishing line.

I managed to grab it, but it was hard to hang on to. I debated with myself: would I wrap the line around my little finger – perhaps killing the finger to save my life?

Jeff was still shrieking frantically at me. 'Haul yourself in, David. For God's sake, haul yourself in!'

'I can't. I haven't got the strength,' I gasped back, trying not to swallow too much of the salty water in the process. 'Please, please haul me in,' was all I could muster.

My desperation must have got through to him, because slowly but surely he dragged me towards the boat. It seemed to take an age, but finally I was grasping its battered, useless frame.

Jeff proved stronger than I had expected, and he hauled me up onto the sail-strewn stern. I lay there in a heap, relieved it was all over, but finding it hard to believe that I was still alive.

Mike called out from the front of the boat, enquiring rather irritatedly about our chances of rescue. He had no idea of the drama that had been going on behind him over the last few minutes.

Fortunately someone had seen our plight. Though far away, they'd noticed our damaged craft, its sail trailing in the water, drifting with the tide.

None of us had much to say as we were towed back to port. As we finally reached land, Jeff said, 'You know, I was really mad at you when you were in the water. I've never lost anyone before when I've been sailing, and I didn't want to start doing so now!'

I gasped. 'What on earth do you think I was thinking about at the time? How do you think I felt?'

He had no reply.

Dissolute in Resolute

Ryan Ver Berkmoes

Ryan grew up in Santa Cruz, California, where he left at age seventeen for college in the Midwest. He took five years to complete his four-year degree at the University of Notre Dame because the new-found joys of working at the campus newspaper and at a local TV station made such mundane matters as attending class seem frivolous. After a year of sixty-hour weeks working as managing editor for a small muckraking publication, Ryan took his first trip to Europe, which lasted for seven months and confirmed his long-suspected wanderlust. Since then his byline has appeared in the *Chicago Sun-Times*, *Chicago Tribune*, *Chicago* magazine and quite a few other publications with the word 'Chicago' in the title. Ryan is the author of Lonely Planet's guide to Chicago; he has also worked on *Canada* and the upcoming *Texas* guide, and has updated the Germany chapter in *Western Europe*. He currently resides in London with his journalist wife, Sara Marley.

AS the plane broke through the low clouds, I saw a bright white iceberg surrounded by inky-blue water. The second thing I saw was the wreck of a large plane, its torn aluminium fuselage glistening in the sun. Minutes later, while I ruminated over these first impressions, my 737 touched down amidst an enormous cloud of dust on the dirt runway at Resolute, a tiny community on Cornwallis Island in the far, far north of Canada.

I emerged into the balmy 3°C air of a typical summer day in early August, some 900 kilometres north of the Arctic Circle. Waiting at the bottom of the rickety portable stairs was the group of passengers who would fly back with the plane to Yellowknife, the capital of the Northwest Territories, 1500 kilometres to the south-west. Most were members of an eco-tourist group, clad in the bright red parkas they were required to wear should they wander off into the Arctic.

I scarcely noted their jovial spirits, little realising that just forty-eight hours later I would enviously recall these chuckling, red-suited tourists who'd been able to leave Resolute.

I left the hovel that passed for Resolute's air terminal, and took stock of the immediate town, a small collection of huts and low buildings which definitely put the shack in ram*shack*le. In the distance I spotted my lodgings, the Narwhal Inn: a central Quonset hut, from which branched several wings designed to conform with the local style of shack. For this I was paying more than two hundred dollars a night? I wasn't really surprised, given my previous trips to the Arctic, where the metres of permafrost precluded any sort of foundations and all building materials had to be imported at tremendous cost.

Once inside I met Tom the manager, who seemed in a bit of a rush as he checked me in. His cheerful jabber was brought up short, however, when I made my standard request for a 'nice bright room with good light'. After a pause, Tom said, 'Your room doesn't have a window.' To show my pluck, I quickly responded, 'Well, I won't have to worry about drapes then.'

'That's the spirit!' Tom proclaimed. I asked if he'd have a minute to answer a few questions about Resolute, but he demurred, explaining that his six-week shift was over and he had to race to get on the plane I'd just flown in on. 'But my replacement will be happy to talk,' he said, grabbing his bag and dashing out the door.

Upstairs I quickly decided why there wasn't a window in my room: the décor's colour scheme of brown accented with grey would have absorbed any natural light. As it was, the buzzing fluorescent light could only lend a greenish glare to the mismatched, cigarette-burned furniture.

This wasn't a place to linger. Back in the 'lobby', Tom's predictions of his replacement's volubility proved to be erroneous. The newly arrived Ned sat slumped in a chair idly paging through some of Tom's notes. I asked him what were the highlights of Resolute. 'Nothing.' How about things to do? 'Nothing.' Things to see? 'Nothing.' I was about to ask him if there were places I could go, but thought better of it. Trying a little matey charm, I enquired, 'Guess you're not thrilled to be back at work?' Ned replied glumly, 'How'd you like to be here for six weeks?'

It was time to explore Resolute on my own. Stepping out into the cold air, I wondered if all the Narwhal's managers were like Ned at the start of their shift and like Tom at the end.

The gently undulating terrain stretched away in all directions. As I gazed at the bleak vista of greyish-brown rocks that was actually a brighter shade than my room, it dawned on me why I'd felt a vague familiarity with the scenery ever since my first glimpse from the plane: it was just like the moon! Every picture taken by the astronauts that I'd seen in *National Geographic* as a child (in between the equally fascinating features about places where the women went topless) showed a terrain much like this. Darken the Resolute sky, get rid of the ocean in the distance, and I could be peering out of a spacesuit helmet saying things like: 'Hey Neil, there's a basalt rock!' or 'Buzz, this stone's a billion years old!'

I decided to go for a hike to the plane wreck I'd seen on the way in. Picking my way along Resolute's rocky landscape, I was pretty sure that forty-eight hours would be more than sufficient time to gather all the facts I needed. Previous editions of *Canada* had omitted Resolute, which has a population of under 200, is dark from November to February, has no Places to Eat, no Entertainment, limited Things to See & Do and just two Places to Stay, one of which I had already experienced for too long, and that had been about ten minutes.

Still, there was some value in adding it to the book. Resolute is the northernmost place in the world with a scheduled air service, meaning that anyone with the $1200 airfare who wants to drop in for a look can do so. It's also the place where trips to the North Poles – geographic and magnetic – begin, as well as the increasingly popular treks on Ellesmere Island.

I plodded along over the rocks. In the distance the Parry Channel was deep blue with flecks of white from the remaining icebergs. For over ten months a year these waters were frozen. Explorers had sailed into the area during the brief thaw, searching for the rumoured Northwest Passage. One of the most fabled, the Franklin Expedition, had sailed past Cornwallis Island in 1846 on its ill-fated voyage, which none of the 105 crew had survived. The few traces of Franklin and his men could still be found on the shores of islands in the region – mostly empty cans of salt beef, which when exhausted meant starvation. In the succeeding years, waves of British teams had explored the area, futilely looking for any survivors. Resolute was named for one of the ships in these parties.

The crashed plane slowly came into view, and I soon discovered one of the many navigational problems that have plagued explorers of featureless places, whether the desert or the moon: without trees or other landmarks, it's very hard to judge distance. The plane appeared to be about a ten-minute walk. After ten minutes it still looked like it was a ten-minute walk. This continued until I reached it after about an hour.

The plane was some sort of large propeller-driven transport. From various stencils it was clear it had crashed about fifty years previously. Except for the fact that it had been torn into several pieces by the crash, it had been well preserved by the cold weather – as if it had been stuck in the freezer.

On some nearby rocks there was proof that even this hopeless landscape was not totally devoid of life: tiny plants were growing under the shelter of the breadloaf-sized rocks. These tenacious little suckers spent much of their lives frozen until the summer thaw, when their metabolism went into overdrive to produce a new leaf the size of a pencil tip.

It was getting late, but I wasn't worried about it getting dark since the first sunset wasn't going to happen for another week. I *was* worried about some low black clouds that had blown over the top of a ridge. As I retraced my steps, a snow squall suddenly hit and flakes tore across horizontally from left to right. After a couple of minutes, the sun came out for an instant and then the flakes began to blow once again from right to left. It was my first taste of the volatile weather that's the norm at the 75th parallel.

It seemed like a good idea to stop by the airport and check on my flight out. Inside the terminal shack, the agent was listening passively to the rants of a tour leader whose group had flown in with me. The problem was that their planned trek on Ellesmere Island was now in jeopardy because the airline had lost the bag containing most of their food. With trail food not in the inventory of the one tiny store serving Resolute, the tour leader was apoplectic. 'I saw the bag being loaded in Yellowknife and we flew straight here. Where could it go!?!' The agent's expression could politely be described as 'shit happens'. His answers were roughly the same.

I listened idly as the tour leader grasped at the straws of a solution. 'Okay, how soon can I get another shipment flown up here?'

The agent's answer snapped me to attention. 'You can't. The instrument landing system got busted and there might not be any planes in for days.'

Now I was at the battered counter with the tour leader trying to suppress a wild look in my eyes and saying with unsuppressed urgency, 'Wh-wh-what do you mean?'

With the same 'shit-happens' demeanour, the agent patiently explained that the ILS had broken the previous week but was now fixed.

'So then what's the problem?!?' we demanded.

The agent's expression went from 'shit happens' to 'shut up', though he relented to explain that a Canadian government plane had to come in so that the newly repaired ILS system could be certified and it could only do that in good visual flying conditions. 'The planes won't leave Yellowknife if the weather isn't perfect here, and if anything changes during the two-hour flight up, they'll turn back. And the weather changes a lot!' he said, accompanied by his first smile. 'Your plane in today was the first one for a week.'

So the sunny weather that had greeted me in Resolute was a mere fortuitous anomaly that had allowed me to arrive. As I walked back to the Narwhal, I did my best to maintain a Pollyanna outlook: 'Well, I'm not scheduled to leave for two days and the weather's bound to get sunny again.' I might as well have whistled 'Dixie'. The snow squalls had been replaced by a thick fog that not only looked incompatible with flying but seemed to be concentrated on the airport.

My first night at the Narwhal didn't give me cause to voluntarily extend my stay. The hefty fee included all meals, which were served buffet style. The choices ranged from grey roast beef, glutinous macaroni and cheese liberally spiced with bits of pork, and lettuce whose shade of brown would have looked much better on the roast beef. I opted for the soup, which to my palate tasted like Cream of Salt.

My fellow lodgers were divided into two camps: a large number of burly oil-field workers, who to a man gave me malevolent stares as I neared them with my dinner tray, and a group of French trekkers recently returned from a spiritual journey through the northern reaches of Cornwallis Island. I chose a table between the two and had a choice of conversation to listen in on. From the workers came a steady stream of sentences that began with 'Goddamnfuckingsonsofbitches . . .' The subjects involved bosses, 'greenhorn' colleagues, bureaucrats, ex-wives and liberals. It was soon apparent that anyone slightly to the left of Attila the Hun was a 'liberal'.

Meanwhile, the French were lounging around in customised Gore-Tex and Polartec outfits whose cost would have kept a backpacker in hostels for a year. They seemed to have absorbed the spirit of the desolate island and sat in brooding silence. Occasionally, one would say something along the lines of 'Are not stones the embryos of the earth?' To which the others would concur with a round of '*oui oui*'s before slipping back into silence.

I finished my salt and checked out the TV room, but beat a hasty retreat at the sight of that ubiquitous blight of televisions the world over: CNN International. I swear that if I am ever boiled alive in some remote jungle outpost, the last words I hear will be Riz Kahn saying, 'Let's take some calls now from viewers who have questions for the Minister of Widgets from Lower Slobobia . . .'

I finally had to face the grim reality that for the first time in my life I had no outlet for procrastination and might as well actually start typing up my notes. As I found a table near a window that was as far as possible from the 'Goddamnfuckingsonsofbitches' and '*oui oui*'s, I noticed that the fog around the airport seemed thicker than ever. In fact, over the next few hours, every time I looked up from my work another airport detail had disappeared as if a gigantic airbrush was slowly painting the entire scene grey. This was definitely not good flying weather.

The next day I spent the morning interviewing managers at the two competing charter-plane companies, as well as some polar-expedition outfitters. There definitely weren't going to be any flights to the North Pole or anywhere just now, as the wind had died down, leaving the fog heavy in the air.

In the afternoon I began the seven-kilometre walk to the village area of Resolute. This was where most of the people lived and where Canadian government services such as the school, police station and health clinic were located. It was also the home of Resolute's other hotel, which I was anxious to compare to the Narwhal.

As I'd been told, the first vehicle heading my way stopped to offer me a ride. The driver turned out to be Kathy, manager of the Narwhal's competitor, whose affable charm was in stark contrast to the morose Ned. Her lodge, the Tudjaat Inn, had common areas more like those in a suburban home and bedrooms with windows. The lodgers were a genial lot that included Maurice, a government park planner, and Dick, a journalist from England.

I'd already committed myself to a second night at the Narwhal, and for the briefest of moments was sorry I wouldn't have a chance to stay at the Tudjaat Inn. Needless to say, I'd forgotten the old maxim about being careful what one wishes for lest it come true.

Kathy proved to be one of the best ambassadors Resolute could have hoped for. She showed me around the village, which mostly consisted of houses of fairly decent construction that didn't share their architectural heritage with the shacks around the airport. However, they did have one common characteristic. In rural North America, country folk often have old pick-up trucks in various stages of disassembly and parts of farm implements parked around their houses. Here in the Arctic, the Inuit had parts of various critters scattered around their houses. One place might have a musk ox head, another a part of an elk and still another the leg of a polar bear. All watched over by the energetic and snarling dogs that pull sleds through the long winters.

We drove down to the shore, where Kathy showed me some ancient camp sites of the Thule people, predecessors of the Inuit who lived in the high Arctic a thousand years ago. These rings of stone were all that remained of the last people to willingly choose to live in Resolute.

Kathy drove me back to the Narwhal, where the fog intensified the closer we got to the airport. She confirmed my suspicion that the airport had been unwittingly built on a bluff with the worst weather on the island.

That night I once again did my level best to ignore the 'Goddamnfuckingsonsofbitches' and '*oui oui*' choruses. My concerns about escaping Resolute increased with the fog. The bleak nature of the place literally made minutes pass like hours, on top of which my Arctic research schedule for the coming weeks was built like a house of cards. If I missed just one once-a-week flight from Yellowknife, the entire schedule would collapse. Looking about the Narwhal, I tried to decide whether I'd soon be muttering: 'Goddamnfuckingsonsofbitches' or '*oui oui*'. Or maybe I'd just turn into a CNN zombie.

In the morning I peered anxiously across to the airport. A couple of the previously obscured shacks had reappeared. Perhaps there was hope for the jet from Yellowknife! I bid a fond farewell to Ned and ignored his funereal response: 'You'll be back.'

The terminal shack was packed with about forty people. It was hours before the flight was due but an unconscious desire to will the plane into existence had drawn people to the airport. The French sat glumly in one corner and a couple of the oil-field workers provided a profane commentary. The tour leader and his charges prayed for the arrival of their food. Several Americans were the saddest of the lot, however. They had arrived in Resolute almost two weeks before on their way to a long-planned Ellesmere Island trek, but the airport's instrument problems had prevented them from getting any further. Whenever the weather had allowed planes to fly, the priority had been to get supplies to the far-flung research camps and to retrieve trekkers awaiting pick-up. Every time the Americans had been told that the next flight would be theirs, the weather had gone to hell and they'd gone to the back of the line.

For twelve days they had camped in a little wind-blown warren of tents out on the rocks, spending their days at the airport waiting for news of flights. The time had taken its toll and now they had decided to give up and head south. Some lay on the floor in private funks, others uttered epitaphs to the gods and the weather, while the most worrisome cases cackled away with bug-eyed mania. 'Shoot me before I reach that stage,' I thought.

About every thirty seconds, somebody would ask the agent a variation of 'Will the plane come?' Running out of glib obfuscations, he finally announced to the shack: 'For the plane to land it will have to be clear enough for you to see the green hangar across the tarmac.' Forty sets of eyes immediately peered into the grey looking for anything green. Over the next two hours, few averted their attention from the windows.

The conversations were predictable:

'I think it's getting brighter.'

'That's because you took off your sunglasses.'

'I see the hangar!'

'It's the truck ten feet away.'

'Goddamnfuckingsonsofbitches.'

'*Merde.*'

When one of the bug-eyed Americans shouted, 'I see a banana tree!', there was general movement to the other end of the shack.

The reverie broke when the agent's phone rang, and attention shifted from the windows to his face as he murmured: 'Right, yes, okay, thanks.' Looking around at the plaintive faces, he grabbed his bag, yelled, 'They've given up for today. We'll try again tomorrow,' and darted out the door.

Amidst a collective groan of anguish I spotted Kathy. I ran over and asked if she had room for me, since I was damned if I was going to return to the unwelcoming arms of Ned. Thankfully, I secured her last room.

We drove back to the village to find chaos and commotion. A pod of about thirty beluga whales had swum into the village cove from the Parry Channel. That was a big mistake, because the beluga is one of the most prized sources of food for the Inuit. In a good year, the villagers might manage to kill three or four of the whales in long and dangerous hunts in the open water. Here, almost three dozen had virtually come to their door. News of their arrival quickly spread and the entire town ran down to the water. Some of the men piled into their boats and zipped out among the slowly swimming whales, firing their guns wildly. Others blazed away from the shore.

Bullets were flying in all directions and people dove to the ground as shots came their way. The gentle and slow-moving belugas didn't have a chance, and the water was soon red with the blood of the dead and dying mammals. Using ropes, the Inuit dragged their catch onto the shore. They'd killed fifteen whales, ranging in size from adults five metres long down to diminutive children.

The observers – mostly white visitors to Resolute – stood mute on the shore. There was no such reticence among the Inuit, for whom the kill was a huge bounty that meant each family would have plenty of their indigenous food for many, many months. Butchering began almost immediately, with men, women and children of all ages toiling away to cut up the whales. Occasionally, they would stop to warm their hands in the meat.

It was a scene of primary colours: the white of the whale skin cut back to reveal the ebony-coloured meat while the red blood ran into the blue water. I noticed that the heads were left lying on the sand and that even in death the belugas still had their enigmatic 'smiles'.

That night – a relative term since it never got dark – we gathered at Kathy's for dinner. (The nightly bill here gave me change from $200, and again included meals, but the reduced fee meant they evidently couldn't afford as much salt. Damn.) The time since the whale kill had passed quickly. Maurice, Dick myself and other lodgers had been discussing our mixed reactions to the slaughter. The 'save the whales' rhetoric we'd grown up supporting clashed with our knowledge of the important role belugas played in the lives of the Inuit.

At dinner, I met a lodger named Gail, a writer who'd been covering Canada's far north for many decades. Gail was infamous, if not notorious, and other lodgers had said loaded quips to me like: 'Wait until you meet Gail!' and 'She's something!'

They understated reality. Over spaghetti, Gail talked non-stop about her lifetime of adventures, most of which seemed to be carnal. The detailed stories of her sexual exploits made it hard to concentrate on my meatballs. But hey, I wasn't complaining. Stories about insatiable seamen were an improvement on the Narwhal chorus.

However, if the seeming excess of the whale hunt had left us troubled, the definite excess of Gail's personal life was about to terrify us. Over blueberry crumble, Gail said in her strident voice: 'I was in a plane last week and we flew over a lake that had a hill at one end. Guess what part of my body it reminded me of?'

Without waiting for a response she answered: 'My clitoris.'

At first the shocked silence was interrupted only by the soft ticking of the wall clock. Then, as one, the sound of chairs scraping across the linoleum reverberated off the walls as everybody fled to their rooms. Later, much later, people began to trickle back into the common areas warily looking about for Gail, who had left to interview a village elder. Dick was the most troubled, since Gail had promised to show him her nude sunbathing photos. He revealed that he was going to sleep with a chair wedged under his doorknob.

Most of us were up early the next day, tired of lying in bed wondering what the weather was like. Magically – at least in the village – the fog had lifted to reveal crisp blue skies. But what were the conditions at the meteorologically challenged airport? Although it was hours early, Kathy's offer of a ride to the airport was enthusiastically accepted by all.

On the way, Gail tried a few conversational gambits along the lines of: 'You boys were pretty quiet last night.' But she was largely ignored as attention was focused on the skies over the airport. Would they be blue?

The runway came into view as we rounded the last turn. It was bathed in sunlight. Moods brightened to match the weather and inside the terminal shack many of the once-desperate travellers were ebullient. The French had new verve in their '*oui oui*'s and the oil-field workers' blanket denunciations had found new energy. Most of the Americans were happily chatting, although the bug-eyed ones were still given a wide berth.

The agent announced that an old prop-driven transport was being sent to fetch us. There were no complaints when he added that as a result the flight time back to Yellowknife would be doubled. 'I'll ride on the wing!' somebody shouted. In the meantime,

Gail grew bored with the wait and said to no-one in particular that she was going to the geology shack to find an old boyfriend.

Spirits remained high during the wait for the plane, although there were frequent glances to make certain that trouble wasn't blowing in. Our aircraft indeed proved to be an ancient beast that had just enough seats for the mob. Once aboard, the flight attendant counted heads and discovered that we were one short. Gail was missing. A hurried conference ensued with the agent, who asked the passengers, 'Do you want to wait for Gail?'

The answer was a loud and unanimous no, especially from Dick who was sitting next to the one empty seat. The dark clouds spotted on the horizon as we made our way up the stairs only fuelled our urgency. The plane lumbered to the end of the runway, each propeller creating tornadoes of dust. After a slight pause, we took off to the cheers of the passengers.

I looked out the window and caught a brief glimpse of the plane wreck passing under the wing. 'Its wing looks a lot like our wing,' I thought. But such comparisons were soon replaced by memories of Resolute which were bound to last a lifetime, which was about how long my three-day visit seemed to have lasted.

A weekend lost and found (or how I met the Wheelers)

Steve Fallon

Steve was born in Boston, Massachusetts, and can't remember a time when he wasn't obsessed with travel, other cultures and languages. As a teenager he worked an assortment of jobs to finance trips to Europe and South America. He graduated from Georgetown University with a Bachelor of Science in modern languages, and the following year taught English at the University of Silesia near Katowice, Poland. After he had worked for several years for a Gannett newspaper and obtained a master's degree in journalism, his fascination with the 'new' Asia took him to Hong Kong, where he lived and worked for thirteen years for a variety of publications and travelled to Macau frequently – with and without friends. Steve, now based in London, has written or contributed to a number of Lonely Planet titles.

LET'S just say that it seemed like a good idea at the time. We'd organise a long holiday weekend with a group of friends in Macau, that far-flung corner of Portugal just an hour's sail away from Hong Kong. To say that the plan and the result ended in direct opposition to one another is to confirm that Smokey the Bear does not have private facilities in his forest den. We would return to Hong Kong not as overfed, hung-over and 'bonded' mates but as sworn enemies who refused to speak to each other for longer than I care to remember.

The rogues! The scoundrels! The rapscallions! They know it was not *my* fault. They (at least the ones still speaking) have yet to acknowledge that fact after all these years, but all in good time, all in good time. Just to prove my largesse, my generosity of spirit, I'm willing to accept a percentage of the blame – 10%, maybe, 15% on the outside. Let's just try to remember who organised the whole bloody trip. Who, for example, bought the hydrofoil tickets and booked the hotel? Who had the maps and the guidebooks and the intimate knowledge of where to eat and drink and kick up our heels when day turned to night? Three guesses . . .

Yes, it seemed like a good idea at the time. And that was when, you may ask? Well, to protect the innocent (of whom there are none, of course), I'll say the mid-1980s, somewhere in the middle of the year over that long weekend when groups of southern Chinese (and the odd competitive *gwei-lo* show-off) climb into narrow skiffs decorated with figureheads of mythical sea-dwelling creatures and long scaly tails to paddle furiously for about thirty seconds to reach the finish line, accompanied by the din of drums and gongs and batons.

I'd always been partial to Macau (or rather the 'Portuguese-administered Chinese territory', as it had become known in PC-speak, well before the term had been invented), and had spent many boozy, shenanigan-filled weekends there; it seemed the obvious choice. Apart from the escape it offered from the incessant jack-hammering and dusty building sites that was the Hong Kong of the mid-1980s, Macau had much to recommend itself. To get a stamp in your passport and change Hong Kong dollars into patacas – same exchange rate, same currency, really – and pretend you'd gone abroad after a short boat ride. To ogle at swarthy Chinese – or rather Macanese – people who, despite their misgivings, had more than just a drop of *gwei-lo* blood coursing through their veins. To maybe even meet a real live Portuguese, mostly civil servants, and dull and earnest as these Eastern Europeans of the Mediterranean can so often be. To eat Portuguese/Macanese soul food – salty garlic prawns the size of Goliath's thumb at Pinocchio's, *bacalhau* and sardines at Saludes or African chicken drenched in fiery *pili-pili* sauce at Henri's Galley – all washed down with red Dão or, everybody's favourite tipple, *vinho verde*, the crisp, dry, slightly effervescent 'green' rotgut that most Macanese used to brush their teeth and bleach the linoleum, judging from the crystal mountains of empty bottles rising up everywhere. To drag visitors to some of the top sights: 'bone-cleaning', perhaps, on the roof of the chapel at St Michael's Cemetery, watching Hakka women wearing straw hats like lampshades vigorously polish disinterred skeletons (for a fee, of course – this was not an act of compassion) that had lain in their graves for seven years or so. The polished bones would be stored neatly in large ceramic urns: the femur bone on top of the knee bone, the thigh bone on top of the knee bone, topped by the only remnant that still looked vaguely of this world – a pair of dentures with pink plastic gums. (The Hakkas were nothing if not tidy people.) And of course to gamble at one of the casinos, which is why the ferries, hydrofoils and jetfoils were always so crowded with Hong Kong Chinese. Not for them garlic prawns or fizzy white wine or watching bones being buffed; it was the blackjack tables, the roulette wheels and the coin-swallowing 'hungry tigers' that attracted everyone from mandarins and tycoons to secretaries and housewives with mouths full of gold and braided pigtails that reached to the small of their backs. There were other reasons why people made the journey westward – to visit one of a couple of little shacks on the edge of a rice paddy on Taipa Island, for example, where a silhouetted figure dressed in a tight *cheongsam* with a very high slit would welcome punters (checking first to see if they had any cash left in their pockets after a night at the tables) and quickly shut the door.

So, inspired by our wonderful weekends of the past, and ready for some cod, *vinho verde* and gossip, my partner and I did something one should never do: we tried to re-create the moment. Mistake No 1. We gathered together ten friends who really didn't know one another very well at all (mistake No 2), and set sail.

How the problems started is now lost in a haze of strong winds and even stronger words. Was it perhaps that we'd chosen to visit one of the world's smallest territories on the hottest and most crowded holiday weekend of the year? Was it that no-one wanted to change dollars into patacas after all? Did it begin when it became apparent that almost no-one had bothered to bring along a driver's permit recognised by Portugal (NOT a Hong Kong one, as they had been warned) in order to rent the island's Mokes, those tiny, scallop-fringed convertibles that had all the pick-up of a golf cart? That left just a pair of us to do all the chauffeuring around – and I was going to have that Moke with the red bonnet come hell or high water.

I *did* get the Moke of my choice (after pretty much ending a long-standing friendship because of it), but somehow managed to lose room No 205, the choicest of the lot at the Bela Vista, a faded old hotel (before her major tarting-up later in the decade) on a rocky mound overlooking the Baia da Praia Grande and the South China Sea. Room 205 had a toilet that flushed (though the shower only worked when the ancient staff felt inclined to turn on the hot water somewhere down in the dungeon) and a wonderful colonnaded balcony fronting onto the bay. Yikes, wasn't dear Partner – due to arrive the following day – going to be angry! I tried to persuade the pair of scallywags who'd grabbed the room before I could to swap, but to no avail. That left two more I wasn't speaking to.

The number of seats we'd need to book for an evening of seafood-gouging and wine-guzzling was being reduced by the minute, but plans still had to be made. Would it be Pinocchio's on Taipa, Saludes on the next island down or Henri's, just at the bottom of the hill? The mind boggled, the digestive juices churned; all of them had their pros and virtually no cons. And then there was the fine (if overpriced) restaurant at the Pousada de São Tiago, a Portuguese-style inn built within an ancient fortress – a maze of cool, blue-and-white tiled walls and elegant stone and wrought-iron stairways. But that was probably expecting too much from this bunch of deadbeats.

'I'd be satisfied with soup and a bread roll here at the hotel,' said the dipsomaniac boyfriend of my best friend (at the time), who was always broke except when it came to those two British staples: fags and pints. Which I duly felt compelled to point out, sending Best Friend into torrents of bitter tears and Dip to the hotel bar, with its scary propeller-like ceiling fans and dirty glasses (would that be decapitation, sir, or ptomaine?), for a calming cocktail or three. I mean, whoever actually *ate* at the Bela Vista back then, except for the lurid orange fried eggs, Spam-like ham and ersatz coffee with condensed milk that masqueraded as breakfast?

Meanwhile, in one of the rooms on the less desirable side of the peeling old pile (featuring views of the parking lot), a contretemps of some volume was in progress. A dispute over who was going to get which bed maybe? Had someone seen a rat lurking under the clawed foot of the scratched old bathtub?

My tall, giraffe-like friend G— flew out of the room and stormed up the hallway, the distinctive tap-tap of her low heels muted by the threadbare carpet. 'What am I doing here?' she sobbed. Oh-oh. The effects of the fortieth birthday she'd celebrated just a few days before had apparently still not worn off. Did I know, she'd asked me at least a dozen times, that she'd be fifty in less than ten years' time? I decided to give her a wide berth for the weekend. Six down.

I had a soup (a *caldo verde* and not half bad) and a bread roll alone on the balcony of the Bela Vista that night.

The next morning I remained in the company of just two others – me and myself – and I wasn't really enjoying myself (or me for that matter) very much. I decided to take a short drive in the Moke – leaving most of the others to fend for themselves on foot – over to Coloane, the outermost island, before picking up Partner at the ferry pier and breaking the sad news that we were on our own in one of the crappiest rooms in the Bela Vista for the weekend. Perhaps I'd catch another private viewing of the bones of the twenty-six Martyrs of Nagasaki, among my favourites in that great hagiographic panoply of the Catholic Church. The Italian Franciscan in charge always allowed me to handle the relics – first-class as they were.

But it was a short pilgrimage, with the full fleet of Mokes competing with limousines and delivery vans for space on the islands' narrow roads. By the time I'd got Miki, Suzuki and the Ibaraki Brothers into my hands (leaving the other twenty-two for a later date), I had to hightail it back to the ferry pier, where Partner had been wilting in the noonday heat.

'What's wrong?' he asked, reading my face like a book (something I hated; I wanted to be mysterious, inscrutable, taciturn – three options that never seemed open to me).

I felt myself in a most difficult situation. Where should I break the bad news (mostly about the room, less so about the 'no-talkies'). Immediately, in this plastic-wrapped tin sweatbox-on-wheels? Or over cocktails under the shade of a plane tree along the waterfront Rua da Praia Grande? I needn't have wasted my time worrying. No sooner had we pulled up to the roundabout in front of the unspeakable Lisboa Hotel (imagine a squat tin can the colour of Bela Vista eggs with a pin cushion on top and you'll get the picture) than the *other* Moke came careening down Taipa Bridge, the few members of our star-crossed party still speaking trying to avert their eyes and glance away as Partner cooed and waved. The cat (or rather rat in these parts) was out of the bag.

Sunday morning began with a scuffle over deciding who was going to get the four seats we'd booked on one of the earlier boats back to Honkers. We tried to draw straws; someone (not me) cheated and the contest was annulled. We argued over who had more pressing engagements back in the real world; it was a ten-way tie. In the end, we all just grabbed for the tickets – and I came up short once again. No matter, I thought, perhaps Partner and I could have a boozy lunch somewhere down along the beach (black sand welcoming red tides, but a beach is a beach is a beach – sort of) and maybe take in a little bone-buffing before heading home on Monday morning.

The sky had begun to darken and I could see black clouds dancing in formation off the China coast. The wind picked up and then it began to rain – well, 'rain' is hardly the way to describe the sheets of water that pelted onto the stretched plastic sheet that was the Moke's 'roof'. By the time I'd got the self-anointed Gang of Four to the pier, I (and they, I'm happy to report) was soaked to the bone.

It looked like it was going to be a dull afternoon, whiling away the hours in the hotel bar, reading (and not speaking, of course) until it was time to go to bed, and it was (although the 'Tears of Christ' – a white port, not a first-class relic – was going down a treat). Oh, there were a few diversions: LL, looking carnivorous as he always did (and, come to think of it, a little cadaverous too that morning after, no doubt, a debauched night-time crawl through some Taipa snakepit), cruising a drop-dead gorgeous barman (apparently they weren't *all* decrepit) whose girlfriend then arrived for a lemon tea and a snog. Ha ha. Best Friend giving me dagger – no, Samurai sword – looks, Dip falling off the bar stool again.

I went to reception to ask what time we needed to check in for the morning hydrofoil. 'Where you go?' snarled Captain, Bela Vista staff No 1, who looked like he'd been standing behind the desk since the early Ming Dynasty.

'Back to Hong Kong . . .' I ventured. I could see from the look on his face that this was not necessarily going to be the case.

'No can,' he said. 'Typhoon signal up. Number 8.'

Diu lei lou mou (which can be very loosely translated from the Cantonese as 'Goodness gracious!' or 'Drat!'). That meant gale-force winds of up to 117 kilometres an hour, with gusts exceeding

180! That meant adhesive tape fixed on window panes to prevent them from buckling and spitting glass in all directions! That meant stop signs snapping in half like swizzle sticks! That meant getting hatches battened! After berating Captain Ming for not having warned us earlier (like it would have made a bit of difference), and establishing via Radio Television Hong Kong that what was at the moment an STS (severe tropical storm, to those in the know) looked like turning into a typhoon – a possible No 10 (out of ten) – and was heading directly for us, we got scared. Very scared. With the howling winds outside and the rattling windows within, Partner and I hardly got a wink of sleep all night.

It turned out to be something of a tempest in a China *chá* cup. Typhoon Hal side-stepped Macau, continuing to drop enough water to turn the Gobi Desert into a working farm and blowing off the odd roof, but the signal here never went above No 3. Still, storms in the tropics have a tendency to boomerang (Mother Nature's way of telling us who's in charge here), so the Royal Observatory in Hong Kong decided to keep the signal up – and the boats in dock – for the rest of the day.

The prospect of spending another entire day cooped up in this falling-down heap, watching misdirected flirtations, receiving dirty looks from a pair of eyes just above a read and re-read *South China Morning Post* and hearing bodies hit the bar-room floor, was too much to contemplate. And something else had occurred to me, something which until then had totally slipped my mind: I had an appointment for lunch that day with the publisher of a backpackers' guidebook series called Lonely Planet. His name was Tony Wheeler.

Though I'd never met Tony, we'd been in correspondence (by letter – there was no email and even fax was not in common use in those Dark Ages) over the past couple of years. I was editor of a magazine called *Business Traveller*, originally an Asia/Pacific spin-off of a London-based travel monthly but now fully independent, and Tony had written a couple of stories for us. 'Where to Drop Out When You Burn Out', in which he offered 'some hard-won advice about where burnt-out businessmen can take a sabbatical from the stress and strain', had been particularly well received, with such off-the-beaten-track destinations (for the time) as Colva in Goa, Tangalla in Sri Lanka and Koh Phangan in Thailand.

I wanted to commission more stories like that, but I wasn't going to get very far by not showing up. I had no way of contacting him. The telephones were working (a very loose use of the word in the Macau of those days), but where was I going to call anyway? Did cheap hostels in Mongkok even have phones?

In my frustration and in an attempt to forget the crosses I was so often forced to bear in my short but relatively happy life, I summoned Partner to the reception desk at the foot of the rather dramatic staircase where Best Friend (or G— the Giraffe – I can't remember which) had performed her most recent tears-and-a-foot-stomp routine. 'Let's take a look at the guest register,' I suggested, and he smiled. 'There'll be something amusing in there.'

Reading the guestbook at the Bela Vista Hotel was second only to seven-a-side rugby as the sport of choice among Hong Kong expatriates. If you didn't find 'Ivan Wackinoff' or 'I M Hooker' under 'Name', there'd be 'muckraker' or 'witch doctor' under 'Profession'. But the real object of the game was to try to find two names together that, well, shouldn't have been together – a not uncommon occurrence. The Bela Vista was, in fact, a favourite destination for those in search of a tryst – a weekend of lust or even just a night of unbridled debauchery. Why on God's green earth these partners-in-passion used their real names while listing their jobs as 'harridan' and 'mercenary' is anyone's guess (Captain Ming probably had something to say about that), but we'd seen so-and-so's wife's name compromisingly positioned next to what's-her-face's boyfriend's signature – and vice-versa – more times than we could count. The unwritten rule, of course, was that this information was to be kept within the borders of the Portuguese-administered Chinese territory and never exported. Alas, as with so many rules, it was made to be broken.

At first glance, it appeared to be a very dry weekend – at least as far as the guestbook was concerned – with not a single indelicate juxtaposition worth writing home about. Partner did spot one odd entry though, something we put right up there with the 'straight shooter' and 'Dick Long' above and below it. The entry read 'Tony & Maureen Wheeler'.

'Another joker,' he said. 'Whoever it is probably started the rumour about Tony being killed in a motorcycle accident.' Partner was referring to yet another of those urban myths circulating at the time – like poodles being dried (and zapped) in newfangled microwave ovens and discarded pet alligators thriving in (and now clogging up) the New York City sewer system.

After a day of being cooped up with silent (and apparently former) 'friends' and the relentless drip, drip, drip of rain, I was feeling a little feisty. 'Come on upstairs,' I said to Partner. 'I'm in the mood for a little confrontation.' So up we went to pound on the door where 'Tony' and 'Maureen' were supposed to be staying.

I must have knocked just a little too forcefully because the door swung open immediately and there was, well, a rather surprised Tony Wheeler – at least it *looked* a heck of a lot like the photo of the guy in my copy of *Burma: a travel survival kit*. And wasn't the face peering out from behind him that of the woman whose photo I'd seen just last week in *Travel with Children* in the Hong Kong Book Centre in Central?

So we had our Monday lunch after all, the Wheelers and I, in the Bela Vista of all places. I regaled them with the story of my 'lost weekend', discussed story ideas with Tony and told Maureen about my plans to visit Ireland and maybe even do a little family-tree climbing. 'Plastic Paddy,' she teased. I said I'd visit them in their office in Melbourne later that summer and meet some of the Lonely Planet staff, which had increased to a startling dozen people by that time.

Tony never wrote for me at *Business Traveller* again – either the workload (and staff) just kept on growing or he didn't like the sound of that lost weekend – though I would write for him again and again. But that, of course, is another story.

251

LONELY PLANET JOURNEYS

JOURNEYS is a unique collection of travel writing – published by the company that understands travel better than anyone else.

It is a series for anyone who has ever experienced – or dreamed of – the magical moment when they encountered a strange culture or saw a place for the first time. They are tales to read while you're planning a trip, while you're on the road or while you're in an armchair, in front of a fire.

These outstanding titles explore our planet through the eyes of a diverse group of international writers. JOURNEYS books catch the spirit of a place, illuminate a culture, recount an adventure, or introduce a fascinating way of life. They always entertain, and always enrich the experience of travel.

'Lively, intelligent and varied . . . an important contribution to travel literature' – *Age (Melbourne)*

NOT THE ONLY PLANET
Science Fiction Travel Stories
Compiled by Damien Broderick

Here is a collection of travel stories with a difference. Not one of them even pretends to take us to a world we know. This international science fiction collection explores both ends of the space–time continuum, taking us back to the Crucifixion, forward to an Earth theme-park for android tourists and through parallel universes. In a world where every inch has been exhaustively explored, analysed and described, *Not the Only Planet* provides a refreshingly new perspective on travel writing.

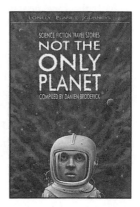

'a stroke of high-concept brilliance . . . easily the anthology concept of the year' – *Age (Melbourne)*

DRIVE THRU AMERICA
Sean Condon

If you've ever wanted to drive across the US but couldn't find the time (or afford the gas), *Drive Thru America* is perfect for you.

In his search for American myths and realities – along with comfort, cable TV and good, reasonably priced coffee – Sean Condon paints a hilarious road-portrait of the USA.

'entertaining and laugh-out-loud funny'
– *Alex Wilber, Travel editor, Amazon.com*

SEAN & DAVID'S LONG DRIVE
Sean Condon

Sean and David are young townies who have rarely strayed beyond city limits. One day, for no good reason, they set out to discover their homeland, and what follows is a wildly entertaining adventure that covers half of Australia.

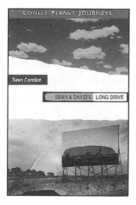

'a hilariously detailed log of two burned out friends' – *Rolling Stone*

'a definitive Generation X road epic ... a wonderful read' – *Globe & Mail*

MALI BLUES
Traveling to an African Beat
Lieve Joris
(translated by Sam Garrett)

Drought, rebel uprisings, ethnic conflict: these are the predominant images of West Africa. But as Lieve Joris travels in Senegal, Mauritania and Mali, she meets survivors, fascinating individuals charting new ways of living between tradition and modernity. With her remarkable gift for drawing out people's stories, Joris brilliantly captures the rhythms of a world that refuses to give in.

THE GATES OF DAMASCUS
Lieve Joris
(translated by Sam Garrett)

This best-selling book is a beautifully drawn portrait of day-to-day life in modern Syria. Through her intimate contact with local people, Lieve Joris draws us into the fascinating world that lies behind the gates of Damascus. Hala's husband is a political prisoner, jailed for his opposition to the Assad regime; through the author's friendship with Hala we see how Syrian politics impacts on the lives of ordinary people.

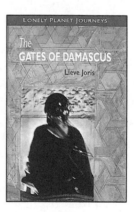

'she has expanded the boundaries of travel writing'
– Times Literary Supplement

PLANET TALK
Lonely Planet's FREE quarterly newsletter

Every issue of PLANET TALK is packed with up-to-date travel news and advice including:

- a letter from Lonely Planet founders Tony and Maureen Wheeler
- travel diary from a Lonely Planet author
- find out what it's really like out on the road
- feature article on an important and topical travel issue
- a selection of recent letters from our readers
- the latest travel news from all over the world
- details on Lonely Planet's new and forthcoming releases

To join our mailing list contact any Lonely Planet office.

LONELY PLANET OFFICES

Australia: PO Box 617, Hawthorn 3122, Victoria
tel: 03 9819 1877 fax: 03 9819 6459
email: talk2us@lonelyplanet.com.au

USA: 150 Linden St, Oakland, CA 94607
tel: 510 893 8555 TOLL FREE: 800 275-8555
fax: 510 893 8572
email: info@lonelyplanet.com

UK: 10a Spring Place, London NW5 3BH
tel: 020 7428 4800 fax: 020 7428 4828
email: go@lonelyplanet.co.uk

France: 1 rue du Dahomey, 75011, Paris
tel: 01 55 25 33 00 fax: 01 55 25 33 01
email: bip@lonelyplanet.fr

www.lonelyplanet.com

THE LONELY PLANET STORY

Lonely Planet published its first book in 1973 in response to the numerous 'How did you do it?' questions Maureen and Tony Wheeler were asked after driving, busing, hitching, sailing and railing their way from England to Australia.

Written at a kitchen table and hand collated, trimmed and stapled, *Across Asia on the Cheap* became an instant local bestseller, inspiring thoughts of another book.

Eighteen months in South-East Asia resulted in their second guide, *South-East Asia on a shoestring*, which they put together in a backstreet Chinese hotel in Singapore in 1975. The 'yellow bible', as it quickly became known to backpackers around the world, soon became *the* guide to the region. It has sold well over half a million copies and is now in its 9th edition, still retaining its familiar yellow cover.

Today there are over 350 titles, including travel guides, walking guides, language kits and phrasebooks, travel atlases and travel literature. The company is the largest independent travel publisher in the world. Although Lonely Planet initially specialised in guides to Asia, today there are few corners of the globe that have not been covered.

The emphasis continues to be on travel for independent travellers. Tony and Maureen still travel for several months of each year and play an active part in the writing, updating and quality control of Lonely Planet's guides.

They have been joined by over 80 authors and 200 staff at our offices in Melbourne (Australia), Oakland (USA), London (UK) and Paris (France). Travellers themselves also make a valuable contribution to the guides through the feedback we receive in thousands of letters each year and on our web site.

The people at Lonely Planet strongly believe that travellers can make a positive contribution to the countries they visit, both through their appreciation of the countries' culture, wildlife and natural features, and through the money they spend. In addition, the company makes a direct contribution to the countries and regions it covers. Since 1986 a percentage of the income from each book has been donated to ventures such as famine relief in Africa; aid projects in India; agricultural projects in Central America; Greenpeace's efforts to halt French nuclear testing in the Pacific; and Amnesty International.

'I hope we send people out with the right attitude about travel. You realise when you travel that there are so many different perspectives about the world, so we hope these books will make people more interested in what they see.'

– Tony Wheeler